30:70
Architecture as a Balancing Act

Sergei Tchoban and Vladimir Sedov
Foreword by Bernhard Schulz

DOM
publishers

Inhalt

Bernhard Schulz

Foreword

Architecture surrounds us more than ever before. Urbanisation, increasing sprawl, and rising numbers of urban inhabitants are not just abstract statistics. They are the experience of everyday life. The desire to feel at ease in our built environment – and to take pleasure in it – is not simply the longing of aesthetes shut away in their ivory towers. It is an absolute necessity. Health, well-being, and, equally importantly, the productivity of urban inhabitants also depend upon cities having a 'felicitous' appearance.

But in our pluralistic society there are different views as to how urban architecture is to be created. Here it is important to note that architecture was once viewed as a given. It was a given in the sense that there were rules that obtained – these rules might differ from country to country, region to region, and even city to city in some instances, but in any particular context they were a given. And it was a given that older, outdated buildings were to be modified or added to. They were only torn down if absolutely necessary. Historically speaking, demolition was the exception; previous generations were aware of how much 'value' a building embodied in terms of materials and labour, and this value did not just disappear. A building could not simply be 'written off' – its value could only be amortised through physical usage.

Modernity, however, has an easy relationship with demolition, at least in theory. There have been any number of radical demands for the demolition of entire cities in order to create space for the new. It was not until World War II brought such sweeping destruction that the removal of existing building stock became a matter of course and was transformed into a tool of urban policy. It is important not to discount the good intentions behind this. Light, air, and sun for everyone: these demands for a social policy aimed at hygiene and a share in life's happiness could ultimately never have been realised in any other way. The oppressively poor living conditions arising from overpopulated and badly built cities dating back to the early Industrial Revolution first had to be done away with if these goals were ever to be achieved.

Over the course of time, however, a sense of unease began to creep in. This was directed at modernist architecture or, more precisely, at the existing architectural environment. The more old buildings disappeared – and often these old buildings were still perfectly fit for use or could have been renovated to make them fit for use – the stronger the calls for their protection. Heritage preservation, originally aimed solely at protecting architectural monuments such as cathedrals or palaces, became ever more routine. Today it even encompasses unremarkable commercial buildings, should their age or rarity make them a member of an 'endangered species' that requires protection for its own sake.

The rather despairing desire – albeit one that is prevalent in our society – to preserve the old reflects the unease we feel when confronted with the built environment.

The average appearance of cities and housing estates – apart from the few distinguished buildings designed and constructed at great expense, such as town halls, theatres, the headquarters of large companies, and so on – simply does not measure up. The sense of the given in buildings has been lost. Both the demand for the removal of the existing that modernism has given rise to and the desire for its protection offer evidence of how architecture is able to reflect upon itself. It is not only architects and theoreticians but the general public too that are giving thought to what is being built and why. Essentially, this has happened ever since architecture developed an awareness of its own place in history. Even the most ancient builders were aware of what is 'right' and 'wrong'. How else could they have built all their Egyptian, Greek, or Roman temples according to the rules?

The Renaissance, prompted by its desire to return to architecture's origins, sought out and found purchase in antiquity. During this time the treatise by the Roman Vitruvius with its triad of *firmitas, utilitas*, and *venustas* – solidity, utility, and beauty – offered a set of guiding principles that went undisputed. But what did antiquity actually look like? This empirical knowledge was gained by visiting Rome and from numerous archaeological excavations. Vitruvius's ideas endured – only 'beauty' was sacrificed at some point, for, unlike the other two concepts, it was not something that could be practically verified and determined. In the twentieth century 'beauty' became taboo: rather than being coyly passed over, it was actively weeded out and banished. This was achieved by declaring that anything that was functional, i.e. usable and useful, was also beautiful for this very reason – if anyone actually dared to make use of such an alienated term.

In their essay, Sergei Tchoban and Vladimir Sedov do not write about 'beauty' – at least not in terms of definitions and historical concepts thereof. They write about the relationship between outstanding edifices and the background structures, the nameless buildings that surround them, or, if you will, about the relationship between architectural monuments and the vast majority of what is built. They begin with the question of the unease we feel when confronted with contemporary architecture but refrain from mere blanket criticism of our modern-day culture. On the contrary, they endeavour to trace and briefly outline the course of architectural history as they pursue an answer to their own question by following a historical and empirical path.

An architectural history of the last 2,500 years represents an unusual undertaking. Normally architectural historians write about individual eras and never attempt overall histories. If they do, there is usually a major lacuna between antiquity and the early Middle Ages – as if the one had almost nothing to do with the other. Another break is located somewhere in the nineteenth century. It might be Joseph Paxton's Crystal Palace for London's Great Exhibition of 1851, some other building displaying purely technical aesthetics, or even the backlash that arrived in around 1890 in the form of the art nouveau movement. What we are getting at here is the arrival of modernism, which became increasingly ill-defined, the longer it lasted, and has since been followed by postmodernism and even neomodernism. A 'conservative' or 'second' modernism also needs adding to the list in order to grasp to a certain degree the true diversity of architectural activity.

But here, too, the authors refrain from commenting. In a sense they take a side-on view of architectural history. Equipped with a deep historical understanding, they also have a feeling – and this is where the terminology begins to get fuzzy – for the rightness or appropriateness of a building's appearance; one could even speak of its 'beauty'. The 'appropriateness' however refers back to Vitruvius, who used a standard word from the rhetoric of antiquity to describe it: *decorum*.

And so we arrive at 'decor'. This is the term that in the twentieth century became a whipping boy for all modern theoreticians, for all theoreticians of the modern. However, Tchoban and Sedov stress that decor did not develop over the course of architectural history into something that was simply 'stuck on' but had, to a large degree, already lost its structural necessity at the time of the ancient Greeks. From the very beginning, constructional logic came up against artistic logic. It has everything to do with the way a building is perceived, from far away and up close, and with the human ability not just to view an object – a building, for example – from far away but to see it from up close, to 'recognise' it, to understand it.

The centuries- or even millennia-old relationship between exceptional buildings – from Greek temples to Gothic cathedrals, Renaissance palaces, and baroque chateaux – and the nameless mass of surrounding structures that provide the visual background to them lost its balance at some point during early or 'heroic' modernism. The architectural avant-garde destroyed this balance when it sought to extend its spirit of aesthetic innovation to encompass all buildings. In striving to provide technological and hygienic improvements, modernism created similar, uniform, and endlessly repeating housing developments throughout the world, a trend that has been particularly evident in residential building.

After a short postmodern intermezzo, which incorporated past forms as if they were taken from a toy construction set and placed them together in 'ironic' collages, contemporary architecture once again began to register a difference between exceptional and background buildings. The wealth of technical and constructional possibilities open to today's architects allow these neomodernists to completely leave behind the rationality and rigidity of early 'classic' modernism. The freely designed architectural icons, the authors write, 'bear witness … to a new range of technical possibilities and a new view of the world'.

Certainly, such buildings stand in stark contrast to their surroundings. The 'Bilbao effect', a term which refers to one of the most influential buildings produced by this new school of thought, has two aspects: on the one hand, it refers to the exceptional new building; on the other, to the contrast it poses to the conventional environment that forms the backdrop to it. And this relationship has for the most part been destroyed. In this book the authors' focus is on the rehabilitation of the millennia-old relationship between outstanding buildings and the buildings that surround them. The question of whether or not the ratio is or should be '30 to 70', an idea that appears repeatedly throughout the book, may be left open; in light of the sheer number of buildings that must be constructed in order to provide every citizen in a given society with housing that is considered appropriate, a far less balanced ratio seems more correct. But this does not play a decisive role in the authors' argument, for the real issue is that both types of building, the 'significant' and the 'mass-produced', must once again enter into a relationship with one another, as was the case at least before the arrival of modernism.

Far from falling into the trap of cultural pessimism, the authors stress the positive nature of this contrast. They coin the term 'harmony of contrasts'. Whereas the exceptional buildings are able to take on any conceivable form, thanks to modern technical possibilities in the area of design, the other buildings, the bulk of what is constructed, have to make do with certain basic forms and basic principles due to economic constraints. The authors categorise the wealth of options available to neomodernism according to five basic building types that take into account their handling of forms and surfaces. The most eye-catching of these are two polar extremes: the one giving visual expression to the construction itself, to the frame of the building; the other stressing its mass and solidity. The former emphasises the building's latticed or reticular structure, the latter its volume. In two of the other types, three-dimensional or sculptural objects can be added to these buildings, or the building's volume can be articulated and presented as a geometric sculpture. The fifth type is comprised of bionic or crystalline sculptures, which refer back to the iconic buildings mentioned above, whereby the completely free choice of form is made with no consideration of how the building is to be integrated into its immediate surroundings. The background buildings cannot be determined either by sculptural diversity or by minimalist reduction. And this explains why Tchoban and Sedov have taken the long path from the architecture of the Greeks to that of the present day. They show how the various eras always developed their own new forms for a building's outward appearance, for the design of its facade, precisely because from the very beginning there was no structural necessity for a given form of decor. And it is precisely the design of the facades, the density and diversity of their detailing, that has been lost in the modern age or was excluded from architecture as being morally repugnant. The authors are not interested in reconstructing the past, as if this were in any sense possible, but in reclaiming the balance between the outstanding works of architecture and the buildings around them.

The authors' side-on way of looking at architectural history is advantageous in that it can take into account a great many things that are absent in conventional presentations of the subject, or receive only a cursory glance. European architecture evolved not only in Italy or France but also on the supposed periphery from Spain to Russia. It manifested outside of Europe as well. It was during the twentieth century – the century of modernism, a period in which the differences between centre and periphery began to recede in Europe before being flattened out in today's world into a global standard – that this polycentric view established the understanding of the simultaneity of the non-simultaneous. Finally, an examination of the 'proscribed' chapter in the history of architecture, that of the totalitarian regimes of the twentieth century, allows us to see how architecture continues to jump back and forth between the eras.

And yet one commonality remains true in the age of modernism, that of the struggle against the old, whatever it may be. Novelty becomes a value in and of itself, even though it may appear in traditional forms that have been readopted, like those seen in neoclassicism's sundry stages and varieties.

And by the end of the twentieth century, this addiction to novelty, something which brings together the most varied and antagonistic political camps, had sucked dry the whole of architecture, as represented in the all-powerful life form of the city. Tchoban and Sedov often make use of the term 'cul-de-sac' in their book. This implies a deliberate dead-end approach, rushing headlong into failure with eyes open. This is not just the preserve of politics but applies to the world of architecture as well.

And so it is that when we reach the end of Tchoban and Sedov's essay, we can look back and see that the book represents a form of recollection, of harking back. It was necessary to observe the architectural developments as they progressed from their beginnings some 2,500 years ago in order to understand this end point – the situation in which we live today. By the end it is evident that the authors make no reference at all to Vitruvius's *firmitas* and *utilitas*. In fact, they do not mention Vitruvius at all, yet they carry his term *venustas*, unspoken and invisible, with them at all times. They find it in the wonderful streets and buildings of Saint Petersburg, which they return to again and again. What follows is an analysis, an analysis of the European city written with a sober scientific sensibility, and an answer to the question of how we managed, and indeed were bound, to arrive where we are today, in the built world that now surrounds us. And the sight of it grips us with unease, for we have not yet understood the design possibilities of our time, and we must finally start using them if we are to create a form of architecture that is both satisfying and lasting.

Sergei Tchoban

Introduction

Some readers may ask themselves what it was that inspired us to write this book. After all, there are countless monographs on architectural history and individual architects. When architects wish to introduce themselves to a client, they no longer scramble to put together a folder of photocopies of their projects and buildings. Instead, they routinely just lay a book on the table – a photo album of the buildings they have realised produced by a prestigious publishing house. Piles of books like this, shedding light on the development of architecture, right down to the tiniest minutiae, come out every year. This book, however, has a rather different focus.

To a large extent, it is a personal and at the same time studiedly objective examination of a single question: What does contemporary architecture mean for today's culture? Over the last 100 years, architecture has undergone a radical overhaul, relinquishing many of the design tools it had once had at its disposal. At the same time it gained a great deal, most importantly through the rapid development of technology. The design principles of today's architecture are very different from those of a century ago. But what is it that has changed? Do 'laypeople', not to mention architects, understand the causes and implications of this change? I have been unable to find an answer to this question in books, interviews with my peers, or in the discussions about architecture that I follow closely and in which I make an effort to participate. As a result of this, I have ventured to invite an architectural historian and journalist from my native Russia, Vladimir Sedov, a man I greatly admire, to co-author this book with me. In our examination of the history of architecture and the decisive turn it took in the 1920s, we will cultivate a degree of detachment, adopting the role of observers who attempt to delineate a phenomenon that already exists and is evident to everyone, even if it has yet to fully penetrate our consciousness. We will also venture to offer a prognosis, outlining the qualities contemporary architecture must focus upon if the undisputed aesthetic achievements in twentieth- and twenty-first-century architecture are not to be forgotten.

As tourists, we find ourselves most drawn to historical cities with their wealth of buildings, including works of intoxicating beauty that make up what we like to call the 'background architecture', some of it erected by nameless builders from a bygone age. What are the prerequisites for creating exciting urban ensembles in which the latest technological and aesthetic successes and the key achievements of the twentieth century's great architectural revolution are not merely epitomised by outstanding individual artworks but in which the majority of the buildings that surround them are able to match the quality we find in historical cities?

0.1 **The facades of the background buildings on the Grand Canal in Venice, opposite the fish market**

I enjoy travelling to these cities together with architectural laypeople. When I travel together with an architect, I can already predict my own reaction to a building, as well as that of my colleague, before we even see it. Up until, say, the 1910s, historical architecture was seen as a series of more or less interesting iconographic buildings. These buildings now seem like the remains of a lost civilisation: they leave such a deep impression that we often don't even know how, by whom and, most importantly, why they were built in the way they were. I always have the feeling that these artefacts were built by aliens with highly developed detailing technologies, who simply left the planet after completing their work without teaching us any of their unique knowledge, so that we can neither use it nor develop it further. When they observe buildings from the 1920s and 1930s or from the 1950s and 1960s, architects particularly like to admire the minimalist architectural language and the unusual, often brutal forms of these relatively new works of pre- and post-war modernism – many of them already in a dilapidated state – whose maintenance requires visible effort. When it comes to contemporary architecture, we often only see the new in the true sense of the word, meaning the buildings are only interesting because they are novel – rather like an internet newsfeed. The architecture of twenty years ago receives almost no attention at all, for in the meantime the building technologies and fashions have changed completely. Often the only thing that impresses

0.2 **The wealth of detail on the facades surrounding the Grand Place in Brussels**

us about the latest buildings is the interplay of material and form: their highly precise joints and connections executed using state-of-the-art technologies.

The overabundance of awards, exhibitions, and publications suggests that the general public is obliged to like architecture simply because its creators appreciate it. In reality, however, laypeople view and experience their cities in a completely different fashion. I love to talk about architecture with a non-architect, while driving along the Champs-Élysées, for example, or walking around Berlin. Even the most mediocre buildings erected before the 1920s are a delight, or at least enough to initiate a discussion, thanks to their richly decorated facades. However, when asked about buildings dating from the period since the 1950s, my interlocutors are often puzzled: 'Is that supposed to be architecture? What am I meant to like about that?' Only the most unusual and well-known contemporary buildings can make a case for themselves. Generally speaking, these building stand out not merely because of their materiality, be it concrete, brick, or glass, but because of their actual design. Other contemporary buildings have little chance of impressing anyone outside the architectural profession. It would seem that today's outstanding buildings require a detailed architectonic background – best made up of old buildings – if they are to achieve the desired contrast to their surroundings, much in the same way that the finely detailed surface of a wood fungus stands out against the picturesque backdrop of a rotten tree trunk.

I studied architecture in Saint Petersburg, a city with an extremely dominant historical atmosphere and collection of old buildings. It is important to note, however, that this historic urban landscape is only a little more than 300 years old, and yet its builders live on as heroes and titans in the city's collective consciousness.

At my university, courses in architectural history had absolutely no connection to modern architecture. As I vividly recall, it never occurred to me to consider whether it would be possible to create something as beautiful and finely detailed as the surrounding historical building stock. Our university was located in a beautiful eighteenth-century building, the very first classical building in Saint Petersburg. Every day we entered its imposing entrance hall with its two opposing stairways before making our way to the classroom in order to design yet another shack with posts and beams. Even when I was at home with my family, I would often hear someone say: 'Well ... it's not possible to build like they did in the past, but you have to try and make the best of things in our current situation.' We completed our studies and sketches on the streets and in the buildings of Saint Petersburg's historic districts. We thought the subjects of our sketches were like the remains of a lost civilisation left behind by aliens who had come from who knows where and disappeared to places unknown with no indication that they would ever return. Let me repeat: none of us, and, even more importantly, none of our instructors thought it was important to create something as beautiful – and I stand by the term 'beauty' – as the buildings that surrounded us each and every day. Nowadays this word is almost never used to describe architecture. It is virtually forbidden. We were unable to travel abroad, but the university library acquired books and magazines from abroad. We were astonished to see that the world was moving not only in the direction of simplified forms and the renunciation of detail but was also developing new technologies that made it possible to build new forms and unusual geometries.

When I came to Western Europe 25 years ago and attempted to develop my architecture career as best I could, I was surprised to discover that the questions that had preoccupied me as a student still remained unanswered. If anything, many of the problems had actually become more acute. The intuitive aversion of many urban residents towards their immediate, newly constructed reality had, in my opinion, unfortunately only hardened. And it is precisely these questions that we wish to address in this book by examining the history of architecture without getting lost in all of its details. When compared with past eras, what is it that contemporary architecture has forfeited? What has it gained? What urban landscapes can we develop when we realise that historical environments often no longer exist as a dependable backdrop for experiments with form and contrast?

What is important is that we want to make this book interesting and accessible for non-architects. Of course, we would be pleased if our architect peers find something useful in its pages. Indeed, we would welcome it. But our target audience is the architecture aficionado. We hope that you, dear reader, can gain an overview of architectural history without having to wade through pages and pages of facts, dates, and technical terms. In around 100 pages you will gain a preliminary insight into the world of architecture and can then, if you so wish, use what you have acquired to delve into the professional literature and expand your knowledge of architectural history. But our greatest wish is that we bring our readers a step closer to answering the following question: 'What are we searching for and what are we missing in contemporary architecture and the modern city?'

0.3 **Street in Saint Petersburg: the historical cityscape is memorable not because of the individual buildings but rather because of the sense of harmonious stylistic unity or a harmony of analogy.**

Chapter 1
The Ancient World

While we do not know exactly when or where architecture was born, experts believe that it was developed, together with geometry, at some unknown point in time in the ancient Near East. The first architecture grew out of primitive prehistoric building types and appears to have been characterised by two previously unknown properties: greater geometric complexity on the one hand and creative drive on the other. The pyramids of Egypt, the ziggurats of Mesopotamia, and the step pyramids of Central and South America vividly illustrate the relationship between early architecture and geometry. Without a thorough knowledge of the fundamentals of geometry, the construction of these gigantic three-dimensional objects would have been impossible. The creative drive reveals itself not only in the individual properties of these buildings, such as their size and the quality and quantity of their materials and decoration, but also in their overall effect. It should be noted at this point that creative design is not necessarily associated with the use of precious materials such as marble or the construction of buildings of a certain size; creativity is equally, and perhaps primarily, expressed in the art of embellishing the surfaces of buildings.

Ancient architecture had no sooner come into being than it began to develop its main design theme – the visual representation of load-bearing structures through the integration of certain ornamental details. Thus the ancient Egyptians created a system of architectural order, the practice of decorating columns and the architraves which they support. Their system already included all the fundamental details of the column, from the base to the emphatic decoration at the point where the shaft gives way to the column's topmost member, the capital. If we categorise Egyptian columns according to their capitals, there were actually two Egyptian architectural orders: one with lotus capitals and one with palm-tree capitals.

Let us pause here to mention a matter that is of great importance for our subject. In the ancient Near East, the presence of specific ornamentation was already being used as the prime means of distinguishing different building types.

The next era of architecture, that of Ancient Greece, is so intriguing because Greek culture was a culture in constant motion, vibrant and in perpetual dynamic development. Greece adopted some elements of its architecture from Egypt – or rather, it acquired certain knowledge from there which it

1.1 The stepped pyramid in Teotihuacán.

1.2 **A fantasy on the theme of antiquity: elements of classical ornamentation devoured by time. The exposed masonry on the right and left symbolises the structural basis of ancient architecture.**

began to develop further, initially in practical terms and subsequently on the theoretical level as well. The first ornamental order of weight-bearing columns, the Doric, appeared in the seventh century BC. In this order, the massive shaft of the column is decorated with concave grooves, or fluting, and crowned with a circular, flattened capital, which supports the horizontal architrave and its decorative panels of relief sculpture. This way of designing the column-and-architrave construction proved to be archetypal and survived into various subsequent cultures and epochs but became most widespread in European culture. Here, as in the ancient Near East, the particulars of this new architecture were once again directly related to the artistic, decorative, and ornamental means that was chosen for their implementation. The usual system of columns and architraves had its roots in wooden construction and would not have required an architectural order and ornamentation to improve its functionality. Accordingly, the revolution that took place in the twentieth century, in which all architectural ornamentation was rejected as dishonest and non-functional, could easily have been anticipated by the ancient Greeks without diminishing the tectonic properties of their buildings. The Greeks,

however, knew that subdividing a simple shape into several parts for exclusively artistic reasons is a necessary means of improving the visual and tactile perception of the architecture. For the eye it is not enough to take in the building's overall volume and its proportions from afar. As the distance between the observer and the object of observation decreases, the eye needs additional information. For example, when we look at a tree, we pay attention not only to the – undoubtedly beautiful – shape of its crown but also to its leaves, and when we look at a human face, we notice even the smallest detail that makes it unique. It should be noted that architects used the human body as their model when developing the design of the columns and the rules for determining their proportions and the decoration of the underlying construction to achieve greater harmony in its articulation and perceptual effect.

The Ionic order of columns came into being at roughly the same time as the Doric, taking its name from Ionia on the eastern coast of the Aegean. The Ionic order was distinctive for its sculptured capitals shaped like a double horn with two volutes and for the column base that represented the transition from the plinth to the column shaft. Thus, the Ionic column was a perfect, three-part composition consisting of base, shaft, and capital, which corresponded to the anatomical sequence of foot, body, and head. The anthropomorphic character of this structure can be grasped intuitively. It was not long before the two types of columns were joined by a third. In the Corinthian order, the design of the capital reaches the height of what is sculpturally possible, resembling a 'basket' of extremely decorative acanthus leaves.

All these types of columns were used in different architectural compositions that were to become characteristic of all subsequent classical buildings. The decorated rows of columns surrounding ancient buildings or leading to their entrances can be regarded as functional only in the broadest possible sense. To be sure, both Greece and Rome as well as most of the colonies of the Roman Empire had a warm climate, so that a roofed colonnade in front of a building could serve as protection from the burning sun – although, in most cases, the monumental height of the columns reduced the shaded area and prevented the portico from serving this purpose. However, the most important function of the colonnade was artistic and decorative. It added an element of depth and turned the building into a geometric sculpture of light and shade. It was these properties that led to the incorporation of the colonnade into various different building types all over the world to provide shade outside their windowed facades – even in countries not known for the amount of sunshine they receive or the warmth of their climate.

The most expressive architectural composition of ancient Greece was the temple. It had a rectangular or round central room known as the cella, which was surrounded on all sides by a colonnade. This could consist of one or two rows of columns. The columns could even merge with the wall to become half-columns or pilasters. Along with the temples, other types of buildings were developed: the theatre, the palaestra for physical exercise, the odeon for recitations of poetry, the stoa for trade and community gatherings. The design of these buildings always involved sculpture and surface ornamentation. Greek architecture was in a state of constant development in its quest for perfection.

This constant striving is best illustrated by the history of the Doric order of columns. The buildings of the seventh century BC were still characterised by visually ponderous columns whose number was not fixed. In the course of the sixth and fifth centuries, however, there was continual development towards greater harmony of proportion and clarity of detail. This development culminated in the Parthenon, a vast Doric temple in Athens.

However, the absolute perfection of this temple prevented further development of the classical canon and created the first architectural cul-de-sac in recorded history. The Erechtheion, the temple beside the Parthenon, displays an almost mannerist Ionic order, which is further embellished with caryatids to satisfy the desire for variety and escape from the perfection already achieved in the ideal canon. Here we are given a foretaste of the coming Hellenistic period, which offered a target to critics by introducing an element of arbitrariness in the way the design elements were brought into play.

Both the Doric temples and the other orders were developed at a time when the Greek world consisted of hundreds of poleis, or city states, that lined the Mediterranean coast and communicated with one another. These city states could be democratically or aristocratically governed or be under the rule of kings or tyrants, but for all their political differences they were roughly equal in size and organised along similar lines. And the world of each city state – a small island of civilisation consisting of the city itself and its immediate environs, the chora – prevailed in a similar way against the world of the barbarians, which surrounded it on all sides: by avoiding all conflict with their neighbours, who were perceived as distinctly alien and dangerous although inferior in terms of strength. Like Odysseus, the Greeks outwitted the mighty world of the barbarians and thus carried the victory.

Gradually, however, the Greeks developed a sense of uniqueness, of intellectual and cultural superiority, coupled with the ambition to spread across the world and to transcend and conquer boundaries both visible and imaginary. After the campaigns of the Macedonian king Alexander the Great, a state came into being that encompassed not only some of the Greek poleis (in Ionia) and Egypt but also territories that had previously been under barbarian rule as well as the Near Eastern regions of Persia, Parthia, Bactria, Mesopotamia, and Syria. The architectural canons developed by the old Greek poleis were transformed in this Hellenistic state into gigantic and sometimes extremely opulent buildings. This was the setting in which the king of Pergamum built his majestic and complex altar, the king of Caria erected the Mausoleum of Halicarnassus, the polis of Rhodes set up a colossal statue at the mouth of its harbour, and the king of Egypt constructed the lighthouse of Alexandria. It was an age of large forms and ever more playful sculptural facades. This age not only brought forth new forms but also perpetuated the old and expanded the physical boundaries associated with the tradition of elaborate surface ornamentation.

On the one hand, the Hellenistic age continued the lines of development of classical Greece. All the major, significant buildings were constructed in dry masonry using large, meticulously dressed blocks of stone with an outstanding texture (ideally marble) rather than mud brick or splintered stones embedded in mortar. These were the precursors of the iconic buildings that survive today and account for the 30 per cent quota of outstanding structures discussed in this book.

On the other hand, the Hellenistic age was the first age of globalisation in culture and, by the same token, architecture. Most immediately affected was the design and decoration of the buildings, including profane houses. These plainer background structures, which made up approximately 70 per cent of the built environment, exhibited a design influenced by the same decorative order as the most significant buildings of the era, albeit in simplified form. This created the harmony of analogies, whereby the background structures and provincial buildings were analogous in design to the main buildings, but simpler in structure and plainer in ornamentation. Looking beyond the borders of the Hellenistic world to examine the buildings of Carthage, the Phoenician cities of the eastern Mediterranean, the Etruscan towns, and early Rome, we find a ubiquitous system in which the theme of support is stated in the means of construction and given simultaneous expression, both figuratively and ornamentally, by a column or its low-relief counterpart, the pilaster. The architectural order as a system of visual representation had spread; it was the first international design style that grew to encompass all fields of building.

The political map of the Mediterranean changed over time. Rome grew in power and influence, and the Etruscans, the Greek colonies in Italy, and finally Macedonia and other Hellenistic states in the east gradually came under its sway. Now the world of ancient culture and the Roman state, which surrounded the Mediterranean on all sides, was divided: the west retained the Latin language, Roman concrete, and the huge buildings of Rome and its colonies, while the east was a different world dominated by Greek and the memories of a glorious history that had not yet receded too far into the past.

The history of architecture looks primarily at the western half of this fundamentally uniform culture, while disregarding the eastern half and the important processes taking place there. This account, too, will ignore the east for a while and look to Rome, where ancient architecture made advances in two areas that were innovative and highly significant.

The first step was the invention of the vault and the development of large-span vaulted structures. While the arch and the vault appear to have been invented before the time of the Romans in the Hellenistic east, it was in the architecture of the ancient city of Rome that they became prevalent and were developed further. The vault in particular was based on a new system that replaced the column-and-architrave system widely used in Greece. This new vaulted system presupposed a completely different distribution of load in the structure and resulted in an even greater independence of the ornamentation from the structural content.

The second step was the ultimate separation of all the architectural order's ornamentation from the actual structure: the columns, now stripped of their load-bearing purpose, merely leaned against the wall, while the vault took over the function of distributing the load – and ornamentation became truly decorative in nature. The veracity of the architectural message – if any such veracity ever existed – was subjected to yet another global reappraisal: if ornamentation is purely decorative, then architecture without ornamentation becomes theoretically possible. However, few representative buildings were willing to dispense with ornamentation, and thus a new overall governing principle came into being. In the case of vaults and arches, instead of the large, painstakingly dressed stones in the columns and the entablature on which the load had previously rested, smaller stones or bricks now often acted as the load-bearing elements, which were thus articulated by the clearly superimposed ornamentation. Now the functions of load bearing and ornamentation were semantically separated. This created the temptation to use smaller and more flexible components (or a uniform mass such as concrete) for building and to apply the formal ornamentation post hoc.

While this temptation led to changes in the construction methods, it had no effect on the practice of the art as a whole or on the principle of decoration in architecture.

With the exception of purely utilitarian structures such as aqueducts, the Romans continued to decorate most of their

1.3 **The Colosseum in Rome: the arcades on each level are decorated in the style of a different architectural order.** (left)

1.4 **The triumphal arch in Rome honouring the Emperor Constantine** (right)

buildings; in fact, the decoration became ever more complex and ever more lavish in execution.

Roman architecture experienced two lines of development. On the one hand, it invented and perfected new building types, the planning and execution of which exploited the full gamut of the scientific and technical achievements of the time in geometry and mechanics, and even philosophy. Rome and its provinces were famous for their buildings: theatres (no longer cut into the living rock as they had been in Greece, but free-standing, man-made buildings), amphitheatres, hippodromes, aqueducts, basilicas for legal proceedings, and baths. The masses of concrete in the posts, arches, and vaults, which occasionally bore witness to an almost impudent audacity, were organised in huge building complexes with ground plans that could be semicircular, oval, or rectangular. In these buildings, architecture attained a new level of technical and artistic freedom and possibility (especially in the case of the vaults). This new freedom, which manifested itself mainly in the conception of space but also extended into the realms of engineering,

allows us to speak of the birth of an 'architecture hidden behind ornamentation', or perhaps an 'architecture beneath the ornamentation'.

On the other hand, although Roman architecture went in search of forms appropriate to the vaulted system and the new dimensions of its buildings, the forms that it found – arcades and concave semicircular niches – remained at the peripheries of the language of art. The fundamental grammar of this language was still the architectural order, albeit at a higher level of development expressed in the invention of novel capitals and other column parts (i.e. the Roman-Doric order and modifications of the Corinthian and Ionic orders). The cornices became more delicate, and new forms such as rustication were developed: a visually 'heavier' form of dressed-stone masonry that originated in Rome and, thanks to the more complex appearance of its walls, added a new dimension of dramatic expressiveness to a whole range of buildings. This new order, the entire system of design or decoration, which used various means to visually represent

the bearing of loads and the distribution of forces, dominated the massive stone structures both optically and artistically.

Rome also boasts several examples of the geometric and psychological heightening of the architectural composition. These are the monuments of the so-called Roman baroque, which exhibit a unique dynamism in their concave details and segmented pediments. This unique and short-lived movement points to the potential for subsequent development in the classical design system.

However, the growth of this harmonious system faltered in the third century AD. The quick succession of barracks emperors, the barbarian incursions, and the spread of Mithraism and Christianity – individually or together – brought with them deteriorations in the quality of the masonry and led to the production of insufficient numbers of columns and capitals. Spolia began to appear as architectural elements, and columns from older buildings were reused. In particular, mouldings and capitals gradually became plainer in appearance – an inevitable occurrence at times of low demand, when the building industry reverts to cheaper products. All these factors bear witness to a crisis in the architectural order and in the design culture of the Roman Empire as a whole.

When Christianity triumphed in the fourth century, the architectural order became even simpler and the proportion of spolia increased, but at the same time the ground plans and the construction of the vaults seemed to grow even more complex. The fusion of architecture and spatial symbolism, which was evident to some degree in the Pantheon, continued in the monumental buildings of the fourth and fifth centuries such as the church of San Lorenzo in Milan, Santo Stefano Rotondo and the Mausoleum of Constantia in Rome, and the rotunda of St George in Thessaloniki. This movement towards ever more abstract decoration and ever more intricate spatial forms culminated in the church of Hagia

Sophia in Constantinople, the largest church of the Eastern Roman Empire, which is occasionally described as the first church built according to the medieval architectural system. This is true up to a point; however, in this account we will treat Hagia Sophia as the last, or one of the last, of the monuments of ancient architecture in which the architectural order still plays a major role – albeit in a more generalised form with respect to the capitals and with extreme variety in terms of column shafts. It sought to bring a familiar 'harmony' to the surfaces and rounded corners of the vast structure of walls in which the symbolism of the cross, the circle, the dome, and the window as a source of light was combined with an extraordinary spatial freedom and a geometrical and architectural virtuosity that had no need of compartmentalised harmonisation and still takes one's breath away today. We are dealing here with one of the earliest sculptural buildings: one which indisputably belongs among that 30 per cent of outstanding buildings whose intrinsic form is so

remarkable that surface ornamentation becomes unnecessary. It seems that the 'architecture behind the ornamentation' prevails not so much *through* the ornamentation (although this too is possible) as *over* the ornamentation, reducing it to an auxiliary, subservient role and even rendering it superfluous.

In the case of Hagia Sophia, it is possible to speak for the first time of a building as a spatial sculpture in which the diagonal development of the vaulted form and the unique spatial composition is far more intriguing than any decorated wall within a calmer and more formally rational volume. This example shows that, spurred on by such new spatial challenges and the possibilities they opened up, iconographical architecture in all its manifold forms had begun to break free of ornamentation.

One final remark about the architectural order. It becomes more abstract and more mechanical in the buildings of the early Middle Ages. This means that, for one thing, columns and pilasters often disappear entirely from the facades and interiors, while cornices remain on the surfaces only sporadically. Even the columns are only suggested in the interstices. For another, when columns and pilasters are still present, they no longer correspond to the classical canon: their capitals are either simplified or borrowed from earlier buildings, while the column drums are almost always taken from classical ruins. There is no trace of a regular progression or regular, canonical proportions. This abstract architectural order fulfils its harmonising function. Thus, the articulation of the wall's surface makes it easier for the eye to take in. But even the harmonisation has become simpler; the erstwhile complexity of the proportions has been replaced by the principle of mechanical repeatability. And this is the most telling indication of the death of the classical architectural order. If the basket-like capitals of the fifth and sixth centuries had been integrated into the system of proportional correlation and superposition, the ancient decorative order would have lived on.

But these principles were gradually forgotten under the pressure of social and economic changes, and so the old classical system vanished for good. Here and there in the larger cultural centres, architects remained who were able to create something significant in terms of composition, size, and span but were unable or unwilling to revive the old system of ornamentation in its original complexity. And so the ancient order died once and for all.

In this brief outline we would like to reiterate that the architects of the ancient world, including the world of classical antiquity, were primarily interested in creating sturdy buildings, based on the latest technical achievements, and then applying the obligatory decoration. While the first ancient temples of the archaic period were not notable for the elegance of their ornamentation, technological advances in how the materials were worked enabled architects to perfect the ornamental system. They built a relatively simple structural frame according to the technological possibilities of the time, and on it they applied ornamentation that was not structurally necessary. Later, the ornamental system became increasingly sophisticated, but all these buildings have one thing in common: the representational, decorative forms that were added to them were independent of any structural requirement. The richly carved slabs of the metopes and triglyphs, the multifarious capital styles, the bases, and the pediments with their reliefs and cornices had their own artistic raison d'être and lent the buildings – even if they were simple, profane background structures – a splendid and elegant appearance and allowed them to age with dignity. In other words, if some caprice of history had caused one of the old architects to declare that ornamentation was dishonest, even criminal, then the shift to a pure functionalism and minimalism devoid of 'superfluous' details would have been perfectly possible twenty-five centuries before it actually occurred. Even then, columns without capitals standing on bases without ornament could have supported entablatures without friezes. Why this shift did not happen then, but was delayed until so much later, is the fundamental subject to be examined in this book.

If, therefore, the ancient architecture of the Mediterranean differed from the contemporary architectures of other regions, this difference lay in the sophisticated, aesthetic system of decoration and ornament that defined Mediterranean architecture. In many respects, the evolution of architecture was the evolution of a system for decorating the structural frame. This is the argument we will present in this book in order to call attention to the dubious nature of modern attempts to create urban environments – in other words, utilitarian architecture for a harmonious living environment – without taking this proposition into account.

1.7 **Hagia Sophia in Istanbul: a new sculptural principle of volume and spatial development that appears to have no need of further ornamentation**

Chapter 2
The Middle Ages

The Middle Ages were a complex period subject to many different perceptions. On the one hand, they are described as a dark, uncivilised time characterised by rough ways (hence the 'Dark Ages' epithet). On the other hand, this was a time of ecstatic religiosity which, in all its manifold expressions, especially in art, celebrated the triumph of the spirit over the mundane world. And there is a third facet as well: this was the time in which modern Western civilisation had its beginnings, a time of accelerating development and an important starting point for progress. All these things apply to medieval architecture as well, which was familiar with ignorance (or at least with a phase of ignorance and a dearth of skills) and with the iconography of the spiritual world as well as with technical progress. The fall of the Western Roman Empire was not immediately followed by the rise of a new political unit of comparable stature, and the signs of fragmentation and decay remained tangible for a long time in the Latin-speaking world. The consequences were not exclusively negative. Parts of the empire, and even individual cities, asserted their independence and found a way out of the crisis. They looked after their own interests without losing sight of their ties with the outside world.

Matters were different in the eastern half of the empire, which had retained its integrity and power and became known as the 'Empire of the Rhomaioi'; the name 'Byzantium' (the original name of Constantinople) was applied to it relatively late by the West. Here the political process continued without interruption, which also means that there was no cultural break in the Greek-speaking world.

In the seventh century, Byzantium fell into a crisis that lasted until the ninth. During this period, the empire's barbarian neighbours and the Arab caliphate conspired to wipe this land from the face of the earth. In its fight to survive, Byzantium developed muscle and sinew and a fighting spirit that seemed incompatible with the flowering of its culture, which lapsed into neglect and a kind of barbarism. In the process, the remnants of the system of ornamental order were lost – buildings became smaller and their decoration simpler.

In the tenth century, however, the Eastern Roman Empire experienced a resurgence of strength that soon made itself felt in sacred architecture. The Byzantines had recently developed a new church typology known as croix inscrite ('inscribed cross'), in which the symbolism of the cruciform space was heightened by the incorporation of the cross shape into a

2.1 **Hagia Sophia in Constantinople: Byzantine architects found a solution for the transition from the circular ground plan of a dome to the square plan of its substructure, thus giving rise to the precursors of today's sculptural buildings.**

system of nine cells, with the dome situated centrally above the intersection point. Everything about this highly symbolic architecture was Roman: soaring arched roofs in the form of domes and semicircular or cruciform vaults; a system of shallow, concave niches that articulated the 'body' of the church from the outside and even penetrated into the interior; and columns of polished marble, bearing details borrowed from the buildings of antiquity, that bore up the vaults of all the churches in the imperial capital Constantinople and thus turned the architectural order into an element of the game – an illusory game played with weight that proved to be weightless.

Byzantine architecture can be regarded as the offspring of the builder's art of late antiquity, the continuation of the existence of early Christian architecture. In the architecture of Byzantium we see repeated cycles of ebb and flow: the refinements of geometry recede into the background and give way to inert, unarticulated mass and simple, unadorned structures, but then architecture achieves an astonishing amalgam of construction and exquisite decoration that combines the illusory with a tangible order of niches, cornices, and stand-alone columns – a system that is nothing less than an abstract architectural order.

Byzantium breathed life into an entire family of Eastern Christian schools of architecture, whose influence or architectural principles can be detected in the architectures of Bulgaria, Serbia, Georgia, Armenia, Walachia, and Moldavia. In these countries, the branches of this mighty tree came into bloom. But Byzantium itself had an inherent flaw, a defect that hollowed it out from within and had a particular impact on its architecture. Because it was a wave of late antique architecture in a medieval environment, the main danger was that this enclave harbouring the culture of late antiquity might become encapsulated and isolated in the barbarian sea that surrounded it. This isolation simultaneously created a constant sense of fear and an attitude of cultural superiority. These two sentiments led to the rise of repeatable forms, the continual iteration of Byzantium's own past. What is more, its architecture contained not a trace of temerity or arrogance; there was nobody who aspired to outdo Constantinople's Hagia Sophia. In the absence of any possibility of scaling greater heights, of attaining larger dimensions or heightened complexity (also in decorative terms), only one path still lay open, towards the intimate and refined, a path of high aesthetic and artistic quality that nonetheless veered too close to self-admiration.

The best examples of middle (9th–12th c.) and late (13th–15th c.) Byzantine architecture are characterised by this self-admiration and by extreme aristocratism. It was a heroic narcissism that developed against the background of rivalry with the Latin West, where for some time forces had been accumulating that, by the eleventh century, were strong enough to 'outstrip' Byzantium – and which began to do so with some success in the twelfth century. These were the forces of artisanal, technical, and intellectual progress.

Is it possible to speak of development in Byzantine architecture? Yes and no. While some degree of development certainly occurred, it affected not so much the handling of mass and geometric forms in architecture as its decoration and the design and imagery with which we are so concerned here. Cornices, niches, and entire systems of niches – these things developed primarily in Constantinople; but while they became more opulent, development was somehow cyclical and interspersed with periods of simplification. These cycles of strength and weakness were the hallmark of Byzantine architecture as a whole.

Initially it was the West that found itself in a difficult situation. Politically fragmented and with barbarism on the rise in all walks of life, it was no longer able to sustain normal cultural development, and architecture too felt the impact. As a result, the Western world was compelled to 'forget' its cultural values, as it were; this, in turn, opened up the possibility of inventing something fresh and embarking on a new beginning with a clean slate.

Finding the architecture of the 'Dark Ages' (6th–9th c.) in the countries of the Latin West is no easy task. Since in some areas architecture was under the influence of Byzantium, anything that can be said about it applies equally to Byzantine architecture proper (e.g. Santa Sofia in Benevento, 8th c.). In other regions, the fundamental principles of ancient architecture were preserved (barbarian rule was never absolute) but were accompanied by a simplification and degradation of the classical ornamentation. The fundamentals survived but became either overly 'fleshy' or attenuated to the point of anaemia or were ultimately reduced to a formula with no attention to detail. This applies to the Lombard chapel in Cividale (8th c.), the Merovingian baptistery in Poitiers (6th c.), and the Visigothic buildings of northern Spain.

2.2 **Example of a Romanesque church in Catalonia with sparse ornamental details.**

All these buildings seem to retain the ornamentation of the architectural order as best they can, but again and again they exhibit an involuntary simplification because the architects no longer knew any better.

The realm of Charlemagne boasts only a single remarkable building – the Palatinate Chapel in Aachen, built at the turn of the eighth to the ninth century – that expresses the ambitions of the new empire and simultaneously pays homage to its Byzantine models. It is a well-known fact that this Carolingian church echoes the composition of the church of San Vitale in Ravenna, a textbook example of the metropolitan architecture of the sixth century and the time of Justinian.

The transition to a new phase of development and increasing complexity occurred very gradually in Western medieval architecture, but its beginnings can be observed simultaneously in Italy, France, and Germany in the tenth and eleventh centuries. What we know about it is based exclusively on small fragments and archaeological excavations, since the subsequent architectural phase of the twelfth century obliterated almost every instance of this style.

What do we find in the twelfth century? A new and fully developed style which today goes by the name of Romanesque. The term emphasises its links to Rome and the architecture of the classical city. These links were manifested not in the development of the basilica as a church type, nor in the continuity of the cross vaults, which Romanesque architecture appears to have adopted from Roman baths and basilicas, but primarily in the return of the system of pictorial and decorative ornamentation of facades and interiors – and especially in the resurgence of the architectural order.

This latter returned in strange guises: sometimes as a pillar of excessive mass or height topped with a capital, sometimes as a half-column leaning against a wall. The architectural order was simplified in many respects; the diameter of the columns remained constant, while the shapes of the capitals were simple and often nothing more than a cube with its bottom corners rounded off. The column bases too were very simple, but they represented a means of proportioning and ornamenting the surfaces and the volume, a way of organising a building's physical masses, like a net flung over it to aid the eye in systematising its perception of the untamed bulk of the structure. In addition to the architectural order, the Romanesque period employed pilaster strips: shallowly protruding vertical bands on the walls that have a step-like appearance in plan and created a layered surface. The inclusion of round-arched friezes of concatenated semicircular arches with their ends resting on small consoles completes the portrait of the overall decorative system used in Romanesque architecture.

However, the special decorative order which the Romanesque period had fabricated for itself did not occur everywhere. It flourished in those countries and regions in which the architectural order had to be laboriously reinvented. In France, Spain, Germany, and England, these odd, elongated columns were part of the first medieval system in which the rationality of the ground plan and the building volume, completed by the system of arches, served to create an almost irrational space representing a metaphor for the spirit. These cathedrals, most of them built of stone – and more rarely of brick when stone was unavailable – were a spatial aid for transmitting divine revelation. This was their paramount purpose and their most significant metaphor. Imperial cathedrals in the Rhine valley, French abbeys in Auvergne and Poitou, and Spanish and English cathedrals all conveyed this early, slightly 'ponderous' notion of God in medieval western Europe.

Alongside this utterly spiritual and at the same time architecturally and geometrically sophisticated architecture, there were also sporadic examples of a very different style of building, one that was much calmer, considerably simpler in construction, and far more intellectual in its treatment of the architectural order. This paradoxical contrast of simplicity and even naivety (simple box-like buildings, flat wooden ceilings) and a kind of enlightenment in the understanding or copying of the ancient architectural order accounts for the charm of Romanesque architecture in Tuscany and Provence. These were sporadic manifestations of the movement known as the Proto-Renaissance.

The Proto-Renaissance was one of the antipodes of the 'great Romanesque'. Its core characteristic was not its size or complexity but a simplicity that combined with sumptuous materials and a meticulous, highly refined attention to details such as pilasters, columns, bases, capitals, carved friezes, and cornices. All this formed the vocabulary of an architectural language that consisted of complex 'phrases'. Monuments of the eleventh and twelfth centuries, such as the churches of San Miniato al Monte

2.3 **The Church of San Michele in Foro in Lucca with multilayered ornamentation on the main facade.**

in Florence, Saint-Trophime in Arles, and San Michele in Foro in Lucca, form the highlights of this movement.

It did not come to a halt even in the thirteenth century. On the contrary, the buildings of the Holy Roman Emperor Frederick II in Italy – not only the portal of the famous Castel del Monte but also that of the imperial palace in Prato – show that the ancient forms were actively cultivated: this required the maximum complexity of which the era was capable both in its understanding of the details and its ability to work in stone. The countries that had preserved the largest number of ancient ruins appear to have recognised the treasure they represented earlier than anyone else. However, this prevented them from apprehending the next style that arose in the Middle Ages, namely the Gothic.

The Gothic style evolved almost imperceptibly from the Romanesque, germinating within its predecessor. Its most important elements were pointed arches and cross vaults with ribs to reinforce the structure. These forms, which already occurred in Romanesque architecture, continued in the Gothic style, where they were adapted to include numerous 'details'. The number of these details grew geometrically in both the construction and the ornamentation, which was initially subservient to the construction before subsequently becoming predominant.

The Gothic style developed at a breakneck pace between the second half of the twelfth and the end of the thirteenth century. Its rise was triggered by the fact that the old, early Christian church typology of the basilica had undergone a change. This transformation sought to demonstrate the immensity of the world and of God, to flood the church interior with divine light, and to convey an idea of the celestial heights. Church buildings grew in size: the span of the vaults increased, but the main thrust of the movement was upward. This striving towards heaven was helped by the science of engineering, evoking the image of the Gothic master builder as a master of calculation. Technology and engineering supported the realisation of the designers' plans by developing hoisting devices and the wrought-iron reinforcements without which the desired forms would have been impossible.

The lateral pressure of the walls and vaults was neutralised by abutments, while the compound pier, which was developed in Byzantium, fused with the abutment in the Gothic period to form a structure whose open appearance evoked the dynamic dissolution of the forces of lateral thrust at work within the building. The ribs became ever more detailed in profile and in outline, as though echoing the lines of force within the vaults. All that was left of the walls was a screen framed by piers. These in turn were transformed into bundles of slender vertical supports, out of which rose the ribs of the vaults. The windows with their stained-glass panes were cut into the screen walls with ever greater abandon. The coloured light streaming through the windows and the floating, tension-filled vaulting lent a mystical atmosphere to the church interior – or, conversely, it was the mystical that engendered these forms and ornamental elements.

The striving for greater height, and to a lesser extent breadth, proved to have its limits. In the early fourteenth century, the nave and crossing tower of Beauvais Cathedral collapsed, leaving only the choir, which rose to a stunning height. Nobody was willing to admit it, but Gothic architecture had reached its technical limits. The style arrived in Germany, England, Spain, and other parts of Europe in the first one and a half to two centuries of its 'campaign'. It spread everywhere, even though the tone was set in France, at least during the developmental stages. If any country stood up to France in the field of architecture, it was Italy, where the Gothic style was rarely to be found in its pure form (as exemplified by the cathedrals of Milan, Siena, and Orvieto). More frequent were buildings which, although sporting Gothic arches and even vaults, were much more moderate, proportionally designed, low-key, and rational.

These buildings with their cornices, pilasters, and other forms of metrical and rhythmic sobriety laid the groundwork, as it were, for the Renaissance. In the varied and vibrant world of European architecture, these imperceptible preparations went unnoticed.

After Beauvais Cathedral, Gothic architects made no further attempts to surpass themselves. The torrent slowed to a trickle before it found a new direction: the focus shifted from structural concerns to the pictorial and the decorative. Architects embarked on a systematic quest to achieve the utmost degree of complication in existing forms, especially the pointed arch and the ribbed vault. They built net vaults, cell vaults, and star vaults, which created dramatic illusions striving for external, representational effects – and achieving these effects required a solid grasp of engineering. France, in the vanguard of the Gothic movement before Beauvais, retained its inventive spirit. But the flamboyant Gothic style that arose here was reinterpreted independently in England, Germany, and Spain. The style flowed across Europe, forming eddies both large and small in the major cultural centres, even though it now turned away from extreme heights and dimensions to embrace more complicated, intricate details of ornament and decoration – occasionally going to extreme lengths in these as well. Today, this strikes us as a certain stylistic surfeit, the sign of an imminent artistic cul-de-sac. At the time, however, it was not recognised as such. And we too might wonder why, if a style can portray (or reproduce) the spiritual with such conviction, if construction and decor function so well as a metaphor for the spirit, there is any need to speak of decline – even if the style has ceased to strive for superlatively large dimensions.

But the decline was at hand. It revealed itself in the exhaustion of the techniques that were used and in the difficulty of finding new forms, which led to the application of infinite ornamentation to the elements that had been developed. As a result, while certain new variations were able to arise, it was impossible to strike out in fresh directions or to develop an eye for the new. The tall columns or compound piers, stretched like wires between complex bases and equally complex capitals (especially in the case of portals), came together with high ogival windows and ribbed vaults in Gothic buildings to create a world that was anything but bound for destruction. It was healthy and stable in its anticlassicism. This anticlassical thrust was radical, but its very disdain for the harmonious whole of ancient times engendered a new, dialogical harmony that recalled the harmony of old. It was this possibility of reflecting on the classical architectural canon that proved deadly for the Gothic style. All it would have taken for the old system to come to life again was the repudiation of the familiar canon of forms and proportions.

The Gothic style is the first in which we can observe in full measure the relationship between the outstanding iconic architecture – mostly religious in nature – which makes up far

2.4 **The mixture of Romanesque and Gothic influences in Catalonian architecture**

2.5 The Sainte-Croix Cathedral in Orléans was rebuilt and decorated in the 17th century in the flamboyant late Gothic style.

2.6 Siena Cathedral, decorated with white, greenish-black, and red marble, was once the main church of the Republic of Siena and is considered the most significant monument of the Italian Gothic style.

2.7 **The Gothic Cathedral of Santa María in Palma de Mallorca: ornamentation on the portal**

less than 30 per cent of all buildings, and the remainder, which were devoted to civil, military, and industrial purposes. While we know a fair amount about earlier eras, the Gothic period saw so much construction that a great deal of the profane architecture of the urban environments has survived: whole streets, quarters, and even towns are still standing.

The salient issue for our analysis is the relationship between the iconic and the everyday buildings. This relationship is significant in terms of both style and quantity. Stylistically, it was always the iconic buildings that set the tone, since it was they who exhibited the most complex forms, which were invented especially for these buildings. They reflected what we would call the zeitgeist today.

In ancient times, the temple reigned supreme in the realm of architecture. The palace, to all appearances, tried to emulate its significance, yet the ruins on the Palatine in Rome fail to convey a convincing impression – although admittedly this may be partly due to their poor state of preservation. The fact remains, however, that it was the temple that occupied pride of place in the list of the iconic buildings of antiquity, followed by the palace, the mausoleum, the theatre, the amphitheatre, the odeon, and the stoa. This is what defines iconic architecture: it must be both intrinsically significant and instrumental in creating the artistic highlights of the city. These were surrounded by a spreading sea of buildings conforming to the typology of profane and functional architecture: residential insulae, counting houses, taverns, and market halls that sought to imitate the shapes of iconic architecture. Once again, we see a clear example of the low-contrast harmony of analogie, a harmony of similarity. When simple buildings imitate their outstanding counterparts, it is rare for profane buildings to approach the quality of the sacred or – more broadly speaking – iconic architecture; the courtyard of a residential block or a villa may feature pillars that are very beautiful even if they do not make the building anything special. The architectural order as a decorative principle gradually trickled down into mass construction. And it should be noted that there were very close stylistic links between the iconic architecture of antiquity and its mass counterpart.

Romanesque architecture produced palaces and houses that reveal the uncontested supremacy of the sacred (iconic) architecture, which supplied civil architecture with analogous details, such as round arch windows, tapered windows,

half-columns, arcatures, and double windows. The Gothic style did the same, although in its case the development of the architecture of palaces, town halls, monasteries, and residential buildings saw profane architecture not only using the decorative and structural forms that had been created for the iconic buildings but also coming up with its own procedures in a transitional zone between mass construction (of which half-timber houses are a distinctive example) and sacred architecture. The best examples of secular architecture exhibit ornamentation that rivals that of the cathedrals in iconography and elegance of execution.

In the Gothic period, therefore, we see the complete, or almost complete, spectrum of architecture. It is usually represented as a hierarchy with the stylistically influential sacred buildings at the top, civil and military architecture, which was derived from the sacred buildings, roughly in the middle, and the practical, nondescript residential and commercial buildings of towns and cities representing the bottom level. The elite 'top' architecture, in other words the iconic buildings, account for no more than 5 per cent of the total volume. Another 25 per cent is made up of the significant buildings that exhibit clear stylistic features. The remaining 70 per cent are the great mass of buildings derived from traditional forms. This is the realm of folklore, tradition, and craftsmanship. Ogival windows and ribbed vaults did find their way into this mass form of architecture, but only rarely, and almost always because a form borrowed from the 'grand style' would dissipate in the neutral background of practical buildings not informed with any meaningful functions. In any case, their appearance owed a great deal to their exposed half-timber frames, window gratings that were compartmentalised owing to technical exigencies, simplified ornamental elements, and haptic walls. Thanks to these factors, the background buildings were perceived as a large-scale, detailed, 70 per cent foil for the iconic buildings that provided the accents in the urban landscape.

We perceive the Gothic style in three dimensions. We believe that we understand its 'message', which is directed both at the people of the time and at us. We love its stone and brick forms with all their tension and, we like to think, mystery. As a result, the Gothic formal language – and especially its ornamental dimension – was revived several times in architectural history, notably in the eighteenth and nineteenth centuries.

2.8 **In medieval Ghent, which survives in a beautiful state of preservation, the dominant architectural works and the everyday buildings from various epochs combine to form a harmony of analogy.**

This feeling becomes all the more intense when we bear in mind that the entire system of Gothic construction and decor was obliterated in one fell swoop. What followed was architecture's first attempt to turn back the clock – to classical antiquity.

At this point it would be useful to note that the space occupied by this chapter could just as easily have been devoted to a study of architecture in, for example, South America before the European invasion or to that of Russia before the time of Peter the Great. For all the differences in the autonomous architectural forms of these cultures, they had one fundamental thing in common: the transition from simpler to more complex structural patterns, which was accompanied by the increasing refinement of ornament and decoration. The perspective we have adopted here could be applied to the study of any given architectural tradition; it is by no means useful only for examining that of western Europe. We have chosen to focus on the evolution of the Romanesque and Gothic styles in western European architecture because of its significance in the subsequent return to the classical heritage, which gave rise to a new international style that, sooner or later, conquered countries with highly divergent cultural and architectural traditions.

The process of development from Romanesque to Gothic architecture was accompanied by the invention of a unique system of decoration, and if the Gothic monuments outshone their Romanesque predecessors in terms of their significance (assuming that 'significance' denotes the magnitude of their cultural contribution), it was because the Gothic system was more refined and perfect not only in terms of construction but also – and primarily – in its ornamentation. The cathedral in Palma de Mallorca could be regarded as one of the greatest Gothic cathedrals – and consequently one of the most structurally interesting – but we pay much more attention to its counterparts in Reims, Amiens, and Chartres precisely because they attain a higher degree of perfection in the deployment of decoration.

It was a new system of ornamentation that was entirely independent of its ancient predecessors. The only thing it had in common with antiquity was the complete separation of the decoration from utilitarian purposes.

The functionality of a building's construction or purpose is entirely unable to explain such phenomena as the involved facets of the stained-glass windows, the stone stalactites of the facades, or the chimeras above the functionally primitive gutters.

And in regional manifestations of the Gothic style, in Tallinn for example, we see a much more economical, elegantly minimalist treatment of the decoration and an attitude to the structural elements of the building that would be described as open and honest by today's aesthetic standards. But it would not occur to us to take these peculiarities as reasons to doubt that these monuments are simpler and less perfect than examples of High Gothic in France, northern Italy, and Germany. We can appreciate the minimalism of St Olaf's Church (Oleviste kirik) in Tallinn, but without emphasising its formal minimalism and the concomitant exposure of the structure, we would be unable to regard the minimalist, 'honest' design as a hallmark of quality. If we are focusing on these relatively remote periods in the past, we do so on the principle that the most complex things merit the most attentive study. One might say that decoration is as important as construction in making up the idea of the monument. In an assessment of its quality, however, and in appreciating its virtuosity and its position in the hierarchy of styles, decoration may be more important than a building's structure and even its spatial composition.

2.9　The Cathedral of Santa Maria in Palma de Mallorca, also known as La Seu, is one of the largest Gothic cathedrals in the world.

2.10　The interior of the cathedral of Amiens illustrates the relationship between the decorative elements of various sections: the altar, the gallery, the stained-glass windows, the elongated half-columns.

Chapter 3
The Renaissance and Baroque

The architecture of the Renaissance is the first full-blooded historical example of memory set in stone. As a culture, the Renaissance sought to recall classical antiquity in its entirety and render its every detail; moreover, in the architecture of the Renaissance, antiquity made a comeback not simply as a memory but in the flesh, as it were, evident in the design of the architectural order, the columns, and the portico and pediment, and expressed as an architecture of renewed harmony that established a counterweight to the Gothic system of design. Thus, a forgotten or half-forgotten system of decoration from ancient Greece and Rome made a fresh appearance.

In the Gothic (which took its name from the wild tribe of the Goths), architects, and indeed culture in general, found an enemy that stood for the wild and the disorderly. The Renaissance reached past the Gothic to draw on antiquity, reviving its memory and bringing its design principles back to life. Right from the start, and for the most part throughout its evolution, the new style had many sympathisers: collectors, scholars, and artists. Beginning with the first heroic deeds of Brunelleschi, who travelled from Florence to Rome to study ancient monuments, exploration of the new style was often akin to a kind of archaeological expedition. An architectural monument first had to be visited, drawn, and its measurements noted – no matter how overgrown, bandit-ridden, or inaccessible the site of the archaeological discovery had become; and later, when it came to erecting a new building, this was the monument that was borne in mind. There was so much to be rediscovered: triumphal arches and amphitheatres, palaces and temples. Everything took shape as a new composition – as a palazzo, a Christian place of worship, a city gate, a town hall. Nevertheless, the borrowings from the principles of antique composition, although very important, were not the key to Renaissance architecture.

The most important element here was the order of columns or half-columns itself as a system for articulating walls and as a visual representation of the structural distribution of forces represented by mock or engaged elements. The architectural order was taken from antique monuments and revived for architecture in general, like a kind of overlaid web of load-bearing – or more often quasi-load-bearing – elements that were portrayed visually but had no technical function. This web replaced the ornamentation of the Middle Ages and hence also the Gothic system of decoration, which now came to be considered inharmonious. It would seem that from that point on harmony was measured in terms of how well classical antiquity had been understood. Therefore, anyone with a good grasp of antique buildings and their fragments would theoretically have been able to create new compositions in this newly acquired style. In reality, however, things were rather different.

The history of the Renaissance in Italy was like a series of waves yielding ever higher degrees of insight, with the crests representing those moments when something new was invented out of an interpretation of the old – even if in between there were troughs when no particular discoveries were made. In the second half of the fifteenth century, Brunelleschi rediscovered the antique order and created a number of new types of building, including chapels, with centred floor plans, sustained by the motif of harmony based on the theme of material flowing slowly in circles as a manifestation of supreme calm and serenity. After Brunelleschi, no other city in Italy was able to compete with Florence, the birthplace of this style, or with the Florentines. Michelozzo, Alberti, Bernardo Rosselino, Giuliano da Sangallo, and Il Cronaca all worked in Florence or at least came from Florence. It is sufficient to compare a building by one of the architects named above with, say, the works of their Roman contemporary Baccio Pontelli to see that in this era Florence was the architectural centre of the world. More or less the same can be said of the Venetian architects of the late fifteenth century, who adopted an original 'accent' (above all in their special treatment of stone textures) yet did not have anything fundamentally new to say.

The early Renaissance, which was mainly Florentine, did not yet have any clearly developed set of rules; rather, its view of antiquity and mode of execution were still largely intuitive. Brunelleschi's and Michelozzo's architectural order had an original, fresh appearance, and it was created by artists, not scientists; it was a first attempt to revive antiquity. Alberti was the first to begin reconstructing it – without, however, becoming academic about it.

The whole period of the Renaissance was full of irregularities, mistakes, curious slips, and lapses, yet all of these irregularities were so brimming with sheer joy at the artistic revolution then in progress, at the achievement of clear forms, harmony, and balance, that the perception of this epoch was coloured by the same nostalgia with which we nowadays regard the paintings and frescoes of the Quattrocento masters. It was the 'youth' of a style in which melancholy had no place and minor blunders were forgiven – as indeed they are today.

It was not until the beginning of the sixteenth century that Florentine architecture gained a new quality in Papal Rome that was characterised and inspired by infinite possibilities, potency, and spaciousness. In a short space of time, Donato Bramante, Raphael, Antonio da Sangallo, Baldassare Peruzzi, and finally the great Michelangelo created what came to be known as the High Renaissance, in which the original idea of measured serenity gained a new significance and a new use – as a powerful architecture that was already entirely (or almost entirely) imperial in its resonance. The architecture of the first half of the sixteenth century gradually spread to a number of other regions, producing a whole string of new architects. In the second half of the sixteenth century, the Renaissance experienced a transitional phase with antithetical figures such as Vignola and Giulio Romano and 'burgeoned' in the northern regions of Italy. Andrea Palladio and Galeazzo Alessi still belonged to the 'serene' world, which was closer to the High Renaissance than subsequent stylistic tendencies.

The language of the early Renaissance was visually pleasing but was understood and reproduced exclusively in the places of its birth: only a Florentine, Lombard, or Venetian could transport it to another country – as we can see in Germany, Hungary, and Poland and ultimately too in the Kremlin in Moscow. Perhaps this language was not yet universal enough and could therefore not be learned. The High Renaissance was a more ordered system, and architects in other countries were already trying to learn and apply its architectural language. Lescot and Delorme in France and Juan de Herrera in Spain tried to work with the order, with the superposition of the columns, with profiles and capitals. They delved into this world of rules – which increasingly were written down as printed treatises – of details, and of general harmony. Antiquity seemed to have made a comeback, to have been thoroughly explored. The architect's secret recipe for happiness now appeared to involve learning the science of architecture, including its written rules and drawn forms, then adding his own talent together with a gift for composition and a creative approach to new combinations and forms, which would further develop the architectural order. And then, so the thinking went, he was ready to erect new buildings that were both majestic and harmonious.

However, this newly acquired structure also contained the seeds of its own destruction, which initially went unnoticed. Only in the person of Michelangelo did these forces seem to take active effect, for as early as the mid-sixteenth century, he set about deforming everything: the surface of the facade and its harmony, the clear geometry of the space, the order, and even the capitals. One might have thought that it was the alien power of sculpture that was invading architecture through the sculptor. Or that the master and his pupils saw something in the architecture of late Roman antiquity that inspired them to experiment with the animated, wave-like, distorting form of the classical order.

What we are most likely seeing here, however, is architects succumbing to the allure of complexity and irregularity. While the little Tempietto di Bramante and the huge cathedral of St Peter's were harmonious and (with a few exceptions) simple in toto – in their majestic serenity and their apparently

3.1 **The Basilica of Santa Maria Novella in Florence: the facade designed by Leon Battista Alberti (1470) shows the decorative structure of the Quattrocento.**

perfect understanding of beauty – mannerism, the new style or 'quasi-style', was characterised by a sense of the fragility of the serene, an intuitive awareness of the instability of the majestic, and a sceptical take on beauty.

From all the examples described above we can see that every style, with its formal and decorative vocabulary, always began with an intuitive early phase, culminating in a harmonious, serene climax, and then continued in a more playful mannerist version, eventually leading to the outright rejection of the entire style.

This rejection did not, however, mean that the acquired style could not be revived later for the design of certain ensembles of buildings. This is what had happened several times previously with the decorative vocabulary of the Gothic and even more frequently with the design system of antiquity.

Humanity seemed to be amassing a treasure trove containing a variety of methods of ornamentation and would fetch them out from time to time so that they could be used to articulate the exteriors of buildings and embellish them with details.

Bartolomeo Ammannati, Bernardo Buontalenti, and Federico Zuccari all followed Michelangelo, but they added a tragic note to his fragile equilibrium, producing an architecture of brooding menace, of masks, and of grotesque faces. The columns seemed to be sitting on a hinge, with waves forming here and there; a fluttering and a trembling rippled through the surface, while on the facade exaggerated proportions, unexpected shadows, and sculptural 'invasions' seemingly force us to read this incarnation of crisis as 'literature'. The crisis, however, consisted not in the negation of beauty but in a sensitised, grotesque, tragic view of it.

3.2
St Peter's in Rome, the main church of the Vatican: several generations of great architects worked on its design.

Many European countries 'learned' the language of Renaissance architecture only in the second half of the sixteenth century and thus adopted mannerism simultaneously with the original 'high' style. In the Netherlands and in England the two currents intermingled to such an extent that people even began to speak of a northern mannerism, although it seemed as if these two countries had entered a period of crisis instantaneously, without having experienced a period of flowering and serenity beforehand. This bizarre ornamental language based on the architectural order and in possession of a certain freedom, which permitted irregularities, blended from time to time with Gothic forms, and thus a whole series of buildings emerged that had a certain architectural 'licence'. The Italians paid no heed to this, while other countries bore Italian architecture in mind and in their free play with architecture gradually refined the language of composition and decoration, developing ever new variations of architectural 'rules'. This practice continued in some countries until well into the first third of the seventeenth century. The ornamental style did not arrive in Russia until the late seventeenth century and found expression in the monuments of the so-called Naryshkin baroque.

Towards the end of the sixteenth century, we witness the final victory of the antique order in architecture. Cathedrals, palaces, castle gates, ordinary houses ever more frequently bore the same features: the load-bearing parts of the construction were presented as pilasters or columns, and the elements they supported, as cornices. These transferred the equilibrium and harmony on the facades into the decoration of the interior, where the new style could be found in many variations. If the owners of a building determined that it did not comply with the new style, they ordered its 'skin', its artistically decorated shell, to be exchanged for another. Many cathedrals, palaces, and houses now had their Gothic windows and articulated facades replaced with the new forms derived from antiquity. In this way, many buildings were 'reclothed'. This was the period when people began to equate architecture with fashion.

It was also around this time that a new architectural hierarchy became established. This style pervaded all types of buildings: beginning with cathedrals, palace chapels, and palaces themselves, which stood at the top of the hierarchy of our 30 per cent, the decoration of houses and local churches gradually became simpler and found the simplest expression of all in

3.3 **The Cathedral of Santa Maria del Fiore in Florence is the most famous architectural monument of the Florentine Quattrocento. Its construction and decoration stretched from the 14th to the 19th century. Only an architectural historian can identify the differences between the ornamentation of the bell tower (Giotto, 1348), the dome (Brunelleschi, 1436), and the main facade (Emilio De Fabris, 1887).**

the houses on the edge of the city, in the distant provinces, and on castle walls. But if we survey the architecture as a whole in search of a stylistic unity, we find what is called a harmony of analogies in which all types of building from the grandest to the very simplest display a similar design structure. The opposite of this, a harmony rich in antitheses, in which prominent buildings stand out in stark contrast to their quieter surroundings, is what we have today. This unity is on a scale that never existed in the Gothic period: while the latter did find its way into everyday architecture and utilitarian art, there were types of building, such as fortresses, granaries, and half-timbered houses, in which there seemed to be no place for what was really a Gothic principle of formal design and above all

decoration. Or else this principle was evident only in a characteristic detail – such as the shape of the windows or portals – that stood out from a neutral background. In the Renaissance this neutrality was rare: almost everywhere we find not only portals and windows but also cornices, pilasters (sometimes in the form of pilaster strips without their upper and lower parts), and accentuated plinths. The rules of harmony and symmetry, the great symmetry of antiquity, triumphed all over Europe and spread even to Europe's overseas colonies.

The architecture of the Renaissance was the first but not the last stylistic epoch in architectural history to originate as a reincarnation, and it evolved through the study and measurement of ancient monuments, through the republication of

3.4 **The basilica in Vicenza: section of the facade. The warriors on the arches are supported by columns that are smaller than the main columns but belong to the same order. Round windows to the side of the arches lighten the visual effect of the walls. A new form of decoration was developed for the design of the arcades, the Palladio motif, which was to be very popular for several centuries. In the background, the corner of the basilica cuts into the neighbouring street. There is a clear contrast between the new, ordered building and the more chaotic medieval architecture.**

antique treatises on architecture, and through the restoration of surviving ancient buildings. The transition from the Gothic decorative principle (which is still apparent in Brunelleschi's Santa Maria del Fiore and Alberti's Palazzo Rucellai) to the antique hierarchy of ornamentation ran parallel to the increase in the number of floors in civic buildings, the change in their functions (we need only recall the advent of palazzi with multiple floors and of huge multistorey municipal buildings such as the Basilica Palladiana in Vicenza), and the advances in construction technology.

One might think that the most important role the Renaissance played in the process of fusing antiquity's legacy with contemporary functions lay not so much in the work of reconstructing antique facades and interiors but rather in the opportunity it provided of using the decorative principles borrowed from antiquity to manage the new functions and to articulate the new, larger-scale buildings and thus make them more human. In this way, fresh decorative elements inevitably emerged whose purpose was to unite the contemporary dimensions of urban construction with the achievements of antique decoration. This was what gave rise to the Palladio windows (or the motif or theme of the arch) on the facade of the Palazzo Pubblico in Vicenza and the colossal order of the Loggia del Capitaniato, which was intended to cross a multistorey building with the decorative order of a single-storey temple.

Architects were faced with a similar and no less urgent task in the first half of the twentieth century when the next quantitative leap in dimensions had to be reconciled with antique decoration. They were aided in this by the structure and columns of the Loggia del Capitaniato, which held the facade together while taking little account of the actual number of floors. Here the pseudo-antique legacy with its ability to adapt turned out to be helpful and was almost universally applied.

It was in Italy once again that a new style emerged in the late seventeenth century: the baroque. It formed a dual entity with the architecture of the Renaissance, whereby the Renaissance specified certain forms and truths, even as the baroque claimed just as many forms and truths for itself. The two were thus in permanent dialogue, and the baroque can therefore be viewed as a controversial style. It emerged in Rome as a direct descendent of mannerism, in the Church of the Gesù, where Giacomo della Porta altered Vignola's original design so radically that the transposed accents generated an implied movement in the elevation, suggesting a more complex rhythm in the 'supports' depicted on the facade. This rhythm testifies to a complex world order, in which hierarchy, rules, and symmetry had gained the upper hand, although not without a struggle, relying rather on a contradictory harmony, as is visible on the facade and in the interior.

3.5 Piazza dei Signori in Vicenza: on the right, the basilica (1546–49), Andrea Palladio's first major building; on the left, his Loggia del Capitaniato (1565–72). For the basilica, the architect converted the town hall on the central square, the 13th-century Palazzo della Ragione. Around the main building he erected galleries in the form of a two-storey arcade of columns. This gave the basilica the ceremonious character of an imposing public building.

3.6 The appearance of the Piazza Venezia in Rome is determined by antique and baroque buildings, whose different compositional and decorative principles set up an exciting dialogue. An early example of the harmony of contrast.

The new style was based on difficult, complex, stumbling rhythms, the accentuation of mass, coupled with forms that appear to be virtually in flight, and a sophisticated geometry. A word here about geometry: the Renaissance favoured clear if not simple figures such as the circle, the square, the cross, and the rectangle, which produced a sense of balance. The baroque, by contrast, used more complex forms, some of which had already belonged to the architect's arsenal in the late Renaissance: here we see floor plans featuring a triangle, an oval, or overlapping figures, often supplemented by exedrae, curvilinear niches, wall projections, winding transitions, and adjoining wings. We also find these forms in urban building, in the planning of squares, and in landscape architecture.

The rhythm of the half-columns or the pilasters on the facade, of the avant-corps, the corners, and the ends, of the curved or pointed forms of the floor-plan figures – all of this was intended to reproduce movement, to embody a feeling whose function is to imbue the architectural order with spirituality. This movement was carried above all by religious sensibility, by faith. The complexity of this faith began to be reflected in architectural forms, setting the architecture in motion. This religious 'movement' was then transposed to palaces and parks, but not until later, for originally the complexity of the baroque was applied solely to sacred architecture.

In general terms, this can be likened to the transition from classical antiquity to the Gothic and from the Gothic to the Renaissance. It seems to have happened repeatedly – and indeed, continues to do so today – that, after a certain period of flourishing, a more tranquil style has given way to a turbulent and more emotional design principle and vice versa. Likewise, today we are seeing the revival of simple, more pragmatic architectural forms in place of the sculptured buildings that were still popular until quite recently – the modern-day equivalent of the baroque. Nowadays, of course, these phases tend to be truncated and the shifts are less rigorous, but the tendency is easily recognisable.

The baroque took the architectural order very seriously and thoroughly explored it, studying the works of antiquity and envisioning the details. Yet it did not strive to reproduce the artistic devices and refinements of antiquity but was inspired instead by its own creativity. The power of the baroque – and, it would seem, its meaning – lay in modification, in the continual invention of ever-new forms and combinations: hyperbolised columns, avant-corps, experimentation with niches and projections and with soft curves. All these attempts to create hypertrophic forms together with the ability to show timely restraint took place in Rome. With its two architectural geniuses Gian Lorenzo Bernini and Francesco Borromini, Rome remained the centre of the baroque for the entire seventeenth century, if not longer. Anything that was done in other Italian architectural centres represented an attempt to develop further – in some cases highly effectively (Guarino Guarini in Turin and Baldassare Longhena in Venice, for example) – the most important principles taken from Rome.

At the same time a 'rivalry' emerged among those who had learned from Rome but now put themselves on a par with the city's architects. Initially, it was the French who successfully built baroque churches and palaces but concealed them under the cloak of classicism (although this can hardly apply to Versailles or the Val-de-Grâce church), and later the Germans and the Austrians. Yet until around 1700 the influence of Rome was well-nigh universal.

As the seventeenth century gave way to the eighteenth, a variation on the baroque, the *barochetto*, emerged in Rome, one that converted the freedom and complexity of Borromini's buildings of the mid-seventeenth century into the volatile complexity of the almost theatrical compositions of the small Roman churches on the Piazza Sant'Ignazio. Here the facades formed a kind of 'wave', whose composition of concave and convex elements became ever more complex and sophisticated. This variant shows one of the directions taken by a development that flourished in Rome itself for a while and then disappeared. But in Spain, Portugal, Austria, southern Germany, in the Grand Principality of Lithuania (with the Vilnius baroque), and in the cities of South and Central America (Mexico, for instance) it left behind strong schools, which 'spoke' their own dialect.

Baroque theatre art, which was close to the illusionist wall paintings of the 'curved' facades of churches and palaces and to complex urban and landscape compositions, had a special character. This art transported the baroque into the sphere of the mystical, which lent the already 'undulating', 'moving' style a magical and spiritual touch. The world created by artists from the Bibiena family became more complex and hence ever lighter with every decade until it almost seemed disembodied. The lack of corporeality in the baroque architectural

3.7 The church of Santa Maria della Salute in Venice by Baldassare Longhena: his characteristic free approach to sculptural volumes is the best example of the Venetian baroque.

3.8 An architectural fantasy: imaginative rendering of the Frauenkirche, Dresden's most famous baroque church. (right)

dream became a kind of archetype of the architect's imagination: the early classicists Giovanni Battista Piranesi, Pietro Gonzaga, and even John Soane, the quintessential classicist, were the creators of this airy world of perspectival progressions and casings. At the same time, this lack of corporeality with its turbulent and dynamic qualities underlined the boom that the baroque enjoyed in real buildings: in the works of Borromini, Guarini, and Filippo Raguzzini.

We should stress here that the baroque did not have absolute freedom. Although this style had a number of variants, and despite the fact that its facades were undulating, its contours ever more capricious, and its floor plans ever more complex, it remained within the classical tradition. And this is why no one had yet tried to transcend symmetry, for all baroque buildings were symmetrical. One of the few liberties that the baroque took was to have an uneven number of columns and an even number of intercolumnar spaces (which constituted a serious breach of the clear image of the classical temple, in which there are always an even number of columns and an uneven number of intercolumns). It would seem, however, that this breach was only evident in the avant-corps at the sides of larger buildings. The baroque never confused top and bottom; it changed nothing about the appearance of the columns or the entases but merely played with them. Such games could be dangerous, but they were still only games: sometimes a detail would be enlarged until it was out of proportion, while another would be reduced in size and significance. The architectural order was deformed but not abolished. The rules governing the visual articulation of facades were changed but not negated.

This incomplete negation that manifested in the baroque also spelled its death. No sooner had people begun to speak of baroque architecture as an ugly distortion (and one without any theoretical grounding at that) than the fragility of this style become evident. Moreover, although this was not apparent in the baroque buildings' appearance, architects continued to study antique monuments. The baroque had virtually ignored archaeological interest in antiquity, dwelling instead in its own separate world and disregarding the growing interest in the classical order. This was another reason for the incipient rejection of the baroque. Once scholars and lay people began to pool their knowledge about antique monuments to form a movement, exploring ever-new capitals and frescoes

3.9 **The baroque cathedral in Mexico City, seen from the Plaza de la Constitución: here a new aesthetic sprang up on the ruins of the pyramids and the canals of the Aztec city.**

and continuously striving for fresh archaeological insights, the baroque was left behind, and a new generation of architects eagerly seized the opportunity to discover the architecture of the antique past, which had hitherto not been fully accessible. Northern Europe developed its own, more restrained version of the baroque, as evident in its Protestant churches. It might have been more correct to call this style Protestant baroque, but instead it was given a geographical, non-confessional designation and was called simply northern European baroque. Here the ornamentation and the expressive excesses of Roman baroque were countered – usually unconsciously – with regularity, clarity, and order. In the Netherlands these features of one strain of northern European baroque were labelled classicism, but like the 'Louis XIV style' in France this was nothing other than a terminological muddle. This brand of northern European baroque was certainly not the original classicism, since it continued to display an emotionality and a

rather nervous (or at least accentuated) rhythm as well as ornamentation. All of this happened in what was simply a more austere environment, in the dry atmosphere of rules, precision, and restraint. Residing in the architecture of the Netherlands, northern Germany, and Scandinavia was the spirit of the Reformation. And via Peter the Great's love of the Netherlands and his rivalry with Sweden it found its way to Russia in the first third of the eighteenth century.

The baroque ended very differently in different countries. The style was banished from scholarly and artistic circles in France and Rome in the mid-eighteenth century; in France the baroque was immediately replaced by buildings in the neoclassical style, while in Papal Rome, where little was being built at the time, it was not architecture itself but architectural drawings that celebrated the triumph of a new style. In Germany, Austria, Spain, and Russia the baroque lingered on until the 1770s and even the 1780s but then suddenly

3.10 **The Church of San Moisè in Venice. Originally built in the 10th century, it was redesigned in the magnificent baroque style in 1668 (architect: Alessandro Tremignon; sculptor: Enrico Meyring).**

caved in under pressure from French culture and architecture and from the Roman circle of artists (above all Piranesi and Giovanni Paolo Panini).

Later, baroque architecture came to symbolise the principle of the synthesis of the arts extolled by all European academies. While in the past, too, architects had been unable to do without sculptors to fashion the capitals, statues, and relief panels for their colonnades and had relied on painters to create frescoes, the architecture of the baroque produced, perhaps for the first time, a unity of sculpture and painting that 'resonated' and 'had an impact' on all sides. Mass, volume, the architectural order, sculpture, and painting were subordinated to a will that was at once volatile and mysterious. Nostalgia for this period, for this synthesis of the arts, continued to be (or indeed still is) the fundamental principle for decorating a building in the modernist style. We know the characteristic examples of larger-than-life works of art being integrated into architecture, or even an entire building being designed using the applied arts – take, for instance, the wall and ceiling paintings of the Mexican muralists. In the Soviet Union, supported by the fully fledged ideology of borrowing what was valuable from the past for the modern artistic practice of socialism, this led to a flourishing collaboration between architecture and 'monumental art', which even had its own organisational structure in the artists' associations.

Nowadays we smile when we recall how during the 1980s at the Academy of Arts in Leningrad, the successor to the distinguished Saint Petersburg Imperial Academy of Arts, an architecture student energetically engaged in drawing one of the many angular modernist designs in red chalk would conscientiously sketch in a hint of a collage of sculptures or a frieze in a rectangular area of the facade, anticipating the professor's stern question, 'Where is the synthesis of the arts here?'

3.11 **The colonnade of St Peter's Square in Rome – the work of the architect Giovanni Lorenzo Bernini – combines the baroque elliptical line in the floor plan with exaggerated classicist dimensions.**

Indeed, the baroque created the first really convincing example of an absolute synthesis of the arts, for it was the period when a building transformed itself into a sculpture without any functional reason for doing so and the architect was for the first time perceived as both an artist and a sculptor. It was no coincidence that the baroque was 'invented' by the sculptor–architect Michelangelo, who masterfully designed the staircase in the Biblioteca Laurenziana in Florence as an idiosyncratic, flowing sculpture and brought together sculpture and architecture in the Capella Medici. The baroque produced the first sculptural buildings, buildings-as-objects from our 30 per cent quota in European cities, which represented a first clear hint of the strongly contrasting harmony of opposites. How can we otherwise fail to be astonished at the brutal incursion of emotional elements into a baroque church as exemplified by the antique Temple of Antoninus Pius and Faustina in the Forum Romanum or the contradictory, dynamic interaction between the two baroque Marian churches and Trajan's column on what is now Piazza Venezia in Rome?

3.12 **The baroque fantasy of Prague: in the baroque, sculpture dominates and forms a link with the Gothic architectural tradition. (right)**

Chapter 4
Classicism and Historicism

Around the middle of the eighteenth century, archaeology and art history, which was beginning to emerge as a scholarly discipline, had accumulated so much knowledge about the monuments of the Roman Empire that it seemed imperative to use it. Of course, it was not shrewd husbandry that gave rise to the new and extremely powerful classicist style but rather the feeling or indeed the rational understanding that the art of ancient Rome had not yet been exhausted, not yet thoroughly 'rehearsed', and that the baroque period had taken an imaginary step away from exploring all the riches of antiquity. We should remember, after all, that there were still many treasures in Europe waiting to be excavated – as indeed there were in the Levant (for those brave enough at that time to undertake the long journey to the Near East). All of these resources still lay fallow. Moreover, there was a general feeling of weariness with what was viewed at the time as the excessively expressive and ostentatious language of baroque architecture.

Thus, culture in general, with architecture leading the way, once again began to study the clarity of antiquity that had, as it were, been corrupted by the baroque, not only in the buildings themselves but more especially in the decorative forms. In doing this, however, they did not follow Vitruvius's triad of *firmitas*, *utilitas*, and *venustas* (solidity, utility, and beauty) but found weighty, clever words that are more likely to have originated from reading Latin authors or from the rejection of the Roman baroque churches of the seventeenth century than from actual observation of the antique splendours of, say, the Theatre of Marcellus or the colonnades of the Porticus Octaviae. Winckelmann's quotation 'Edle Einfalt und stille Größe' (Noble simplicity and quiet grandeur) epitomised the image of the new art as a replica of the art of antiquity, which according to this formula was in possession not only of an aristocratic simplicity (a possible substitute for bourgeois sobriety or perhaps even the Renaissance?) but also of a grandeur that, in apparent contrast to the exalted forms of the baroque, had a sedate, more moderate character. Were we to remove 'quiet' and 'simplicity' (as vestiges of the polemic against the baroque) from this formula, we would be left with nobility and grandeur, which would seem to be more fitting terms for expressing the most important ideas of classicism. The evolution of classicism can be portrayed as a struggle between Europe's artistic centres or indeed as a succession of steps in the scholarly archaeological investigation of antique architecture. This investigation was accompanied by a rivalry of the talented, who coupled exquisite forms with ever greater conviction and freedom. Viewed as a whole, this process might be imagined as an uninterrupted series of photos of antique monuments taken from a fixed vantage point – a process during which both the cameras and the lenses as well as the skill of the photographer achieved ever greater perfection, so that the images not only attained a greater sharpness and contrast but also became better works of art as they delved ever deeper into the essence of the objects being photographed.

Perhaps this metaphor should also be extended to the historicist period that followed. In the classicist period, knowledge about antique monuments was gathered not via the building plan but via the architectural drawing (hence the flourishing of graphic art during this period). This also explains the handmade, free reproduction of antiquity in classicist architecture. In the later, historicist period, photography seemed to be the most important medium for arriving at new insights, which also explains the mechanical and even deliberately pedantic imitations of that time.

When and how did classicism begin in architecture? Who was the first to erect a building in this style? Answers to this question may differ considerably. What is clear is that the style probably originated in France, where we find its prime examples in the works of Ange-Jacques Gabriel. In France, classicism was more restrained and austere than its baroque and rococo predecessors, and having come into being under Louis XV, it underwent a very rapid development, culminating in the 'Louis XVI' style.

Italy displayed transitional forms in the buildings of Piranesi and Antonio Rinaldi, but very soon, following Palladio's lead, the style took a more austere direction than it did in France. In the hands of Giacomo Quarenghi, whose career began in Rome and unfolded fully at the court of the Russian Empress Catherine the Great, the building projects gained ever greater splendour and verve. At the same time, England, too, looked to Palladio – and thus prime examples of neoclassical architecture of the most intimate kind sprang up practically out of nothing. The French Revolution, or simply the spirit of freedom that paved the way for it, allowed the French to overcome what the Russian amateur architect Nikolai Lvov called a 'magnificent head of curls' in reference to the Louis XVI style. Even before the revolution, Claude-Nicolas Ledoux and Étienne-Louis Boullée had created a new style, which combined a knowledge of form with scale (albeit with less emphasis on quiet). Meanwhile, the discovery of Paestum began to fire a passion for ancient Greece, and architects rediscovered the Doric order of colonnades for themselves.

It turned out that, alongside ancient Rome, Greece was a very real phenomenon, even if it was initially in the form of Magna Graecia in southern Italy. But architects from Europe penetrated still further, into the Greek interior, and to Athens and Ionia. They realised that Greece itself first needed to be properly explored and that there were also ancient sites in the mountains and deserts of the Near East waiting to be discovered, such as Palmyra and Gerasa, which were Roman in style. The ancient world had thus not yet been fully tapped; there were areas that not only promised new insights but also opened up new perspectives – leading into the depths of history, to Greece and the very source of their enquiry, which seemed to be far more interesting than staying in the middle reaches of the imaginary river of antiquity.

Then, right at the end of the eighteenth century, Napoleon's campaign in Egypt opened a new chapter – the Egypt of the Pharaohs, a period of history even older than that of ancient Greece. The perception of the past became still more profound. The eighteenth century had already adopted many exotic decorative styles: the Chinese, which paved the way for the later enthusiasm for Japanese art; the Turkish; and even the neo-Gothic. This created a whole genre of quirky, playful architecture for the parks surrounding palaces and country estates. New styles sprang from the genealogical tree of European classical architecture: its roots were in the Egyptian style; slightly higher up were archaic and classical Greece; and higher still the Rome of the Republic and the emperors. Some of the intermediate branches – Hellenism and Byzantium, for example – were still unknown to European architects of the time.

Hence the arena was staked out for the next 20 or 30 years: there was a choice between two directions, two models – Rome or Greece. To mix the two seemed improper. All other styles were complementary. The era of Napoleon's triumphs saw the emergence of a style built on Roman foundations, known as Empire, at which point history seemed to have come full circle. But then came Waterloo, which suggested otherwise, even if the Empire style lived on in the German- and Italian-speaking countries as well as in Austria and

4.1 **The French classicist ensemble on Saint Petersburg's New Holland Island is striking in its harmonious monumentality.**

Russia – the two victorious empires. During the Bourbon restoration, classical architecture also dominated in France, but it was precisely here in the 1820s that architecture entered a conspicuous period of 'aridity' that was difficult to explain. The buildings resembled an entomologist's collection in which the many instances of natural beauty are robbed of some of their appeal by their chitinous exoskeleton.

The reason for this weariness of style cannot always be fathomed. Were people tired of the constant imitations? Or was it the new paths and new enticements that were responsible? And who was weary: the public, those commissioning the works, or those creating them? Had the entire architecture of ancient Rome and Greece already been thoroughly explored by around 1820/30? Was it really no longer possible to build new, convincing variants of colonnades, temples, triumphal arches, and theatres in the antique style? Of course it was.

In Russia we see the architect Carlo Rossi, whose classicist enthusiasm was far from being exhausted at the beginning of the 1830s, and the same was true of Charles Robert Cockerell in Great Britain and Leo von Klenze in Bavaria.

Could the classicist line be continued? Certainly. No one really stood in its way, nothing was taboo, and in the mid-nineteenth century we see in the work of Alexander Thomson, nicknamed 'the Greek', a determined search for antique models.

There were two main reasons for the decline of the style: one was the 'aridity' of classicist details that were constantly being repeated without any visible development; the other was that architects were at liberty, and hence tempted, to help themselves to newly discovered treasures or those that had already been accumulated from the jewel case of other styles, i.e. decorative tendencies. This 'aridity' increased further, against the wishes of the architects, on account of their zealous devotion to archaeology, commitment to scholarship, and precise attention to detail. Attempts to overcome this using antique material itself were unsuccessful, so instead architects set out to achieve their goal by transitioning to other styles that on the face of it wanted to be free of aridity. New possibilities were offered by styles of decoration that became better known as Europeans became more familiar with cultures that had no connection with European antiquity, such as those of South America, China, Africa, Japan, and the Near East. Thus, it became increasingly easy

to abandon 'pure' classicism – with every difficulty that arose, with a change in the nature of a commission, or simply whenever the occasion presented itself. Nevertheless, classicism and the idolisation of antiquity continued to hold good, and not a word was said openly against them; but there came a point when they were seen as only one of many possible paths. Classicism now merely occupied a place on a shelf that it shared with a dozen other decorative scenarios.

This period saw a revival of antique decoration, but this time the adaptation of antique ornament to new dimensions and functions was not quite as innovative, since the latter had not changed very much compared with the Renaissance epoch. The architect's role as a sculptor and painter was consigned to the background, making room for him to engage in a thorough study of the fundamentals of the antique order, above all the decorative practices of antiquity. This decoration was adapted to the functional structure of the new type of building: primarily theatres with their obligatory decorated porticos modelled on the Pantheon or the Loggia del Capitaniato in Vicenza (Ledoux, Bélanger, De Wailly, Rossi, Schinkel), banks (John Soane), and large government buildings (which have continued to be copied all over the world to this day), successors to the Capitol, and of course larger domed churches – the successors to the Pantheon and St Peter's (Wren, Soufflot, Montferrand) – as well as museums as a fundamentally new form of temple of the arts (for example, Klenze's Pinakothek and New Hermitage, Schinkel's Altes Museum). This was the heyday of showcase projects featuring a decor that was frequently reproduced yet elegant, and it was a time in which many writings from antiquity and the Renaissance were republished and buildings of these epochs eagerly studied (Percier and Fontaine's book on Roman palaces, Nero's Domus Aurea as interpreted by Brenna and Smuglewicz, Cameron's *The Baths of the Romans*). It was the time of educational journeys, of the Grand Tour, of architectural drawing as one of the most popular elegant hobbies. As an ideal translator from the language of antiquity into the language of the modern era, Palladio was the object of a cult with many devotees. And it was the time in which the western European urban landscape experienced an all-out expansion, reaching cities that, one might imagine, had their own figures to rank with Palladio and could have continued to pursue their own traditions.

4.2 **The Reichstag building in Berlin prior to its most recent reconstruction – an example**
of the historicist neo-classicism of the second half of the nineteenth century

4.3 St Isaac's Cathedral in Saint Petersburg designed by Auguste Montferrand in the late classicist style is the fourth church of St Isaac of Dalmatia to be built on this site. The main reason why the cathedral was built in its present form was to match the ceremonious, prestigious character of Saint Petersburg's city centre, which its predecessors had failed to do.

Until the eighteenth century, Russia had known only ethnic and – in terms of their typology and decoration – original architectural works by Ivan Barma and Postnik Yakovlev, Yakov Bukhvostov, and anonymous architects of the Vladimir-Suzdal school whose sense of how to match decor and construction was quite extraordinary (for example, the Church of the Intercession of the Holy Virgin on the Nerl river in Bogolyubovo, the Assumption and Saint Demetrius Cathedrals in Vladimir, and the Saint George Cathedral in Yuryev-Polsky). And yet it was Russia that became a platform for the spread of French and Italian classicism, above all in the 'cloned' city of Saint Petersburg. In Turkey, too, in Istanbul, where Sinan had once worked as an architect just as significant as his contemporary Palladio, classical secular buildings now emerged. Following in the footsteps of the baroque, classicism now spread to an even greater degree, extending into all Europe's cities and overseas colonies. Thus, classicist decoration with its infinite variations on one and the same portico became the dominant international style and in many regions replaced the original primitive traditions, undermined the diversity of architectural language, and quite soon called into question the very existence of ornamental architecture that followed different designs. Yet, until that point was reached, architecture had to spend another 100 years desperately blundering around as it sought a way out of the tight corset of the classicist canon.

In the 1830s, it was no longer a single style but a way of building known today as historicism or eclecticism (from the Greek word meaning to select or choose) that spread to many places. The architect would simply choose a style from either the recent or the distant past, as required, and apply it with great refinement and, if possible, without committing too many breaches of good taste. This almost culinary art was closely connected with the scholarly discipline of architecture at that time: in order to be able to draw and to execute the forms and decorative details of a given style, an architect had to have studied that style and have a palette of details and compositions at his disposal. As the author of the design and the master builder, the architect had been transformed into a scholar, who had a motley collection of sheets of paper in his briefcase or on his bookshelves, showing a whole range of styles from Egyptian tombs to Roman lighthouses, Byzantine monasteries, Chinese pagodas, and Turkish pavilions. Accordingly, he

would choose a Turkish decoration for the smoking room of a palace, but would use the Gothic style for a Louis XVI dining room or a library.

We should start by saying that the styles were never mixed on the same level or in the same space. They could coexist in neighbouring rooms or in a landscape garden, but there was a certain boundary that was never crossed. We should also note that the architects continued to refine their knowledge of individual styles and the technical possibilities available to them: with the development of historicism, style patterns were copied ever more exactly, and if in the 1830s the Gothic was still being reproduced in a rather generic sense, by the end of the century this style had attained an ever greater degree of precision and historical authenticity in new buildings, referencing local particularities and even a kind of new spirituality that had, as it were, been resurrected.

In historicism the architect transformed himself into a scholarly archivist who preserved the entire legacy of world architecture in his mind and in his library. This was an enviable position to be in: having mastered history and its philological interpretation, he was now more networked and more integrated in the culture than ever. Yet at the same his relationship with painting and sculpture in the above-mentioned synthesis of the arts became increasingly precarious. It was now the architect who was supposed to assign painters and sculptors their place, and it was the architect who specified both the style and the correct degree of synthesis. On the other hand, in this polyvalent approach, a certain stylistic confidence was lost, which made the assignment process and the architect's task of maintaining control over his artist underlings more difficult.

Where was the measure in this mixture of styles? How was good taste gauged? Who was in a position to judge and command under these conditions? Painters and sculptors suddenly seemed to have been given carte blanche to rebel, and the best among them seized the opportunity and abandoned architecture. Those who remained had resigned themselves to working as part of a 'team' or 'orchestra'.

Historicism was a period when many different styles coexisted. But according to what principle were the various elements of these styles combined?

We suspect that all the styles of eclecticism had a single basis, and this basis was the Renaissance and the baroque.

4.4 The Süleymaniye Mosque is one of the most important mosques in Istanbul. It was commissioned by Sultan Süleyman the Magnificent and built by the famous Ottoman engineer and architect Sinan between 1550 and 1557. It is one of his most outstanding works.

4.5 The Château de Blois, restored between 1841 and 1869 by Eugène Viollet-le-Duc and Jacques Félix Duban in the neo-Renaissance style

In other words, during the historicist period the major order of the classicist epoch was replaced by an order distributed over several registers of the kind found in the Roman and Venetian palazzi, in which the network of cornices and pilasters played a major role, covering the facade like a web and giving it a delicate articulation. This web was organised according to a very specific proportional scheme, which originated in the superposed orders of the Colosseum: it was to be found in the columns and was anthropomorphic, whereby the distance between the bands of cornices arranged one above the another changed proportionately with each new level and was not mechanically standardised.

This scheme, this web, which could be used to organise any facade, belonged more to the late Renaissance, but it could be supplemented with various stylistic elements from the early Florentine Renaissance, the baroque, the néo-Grec, or from more exotic styles – and in every case it 'worked'. This scheme distributed rhythmic elements over the facade of the building, register by register, creating a harmonious order. This is an eloquent example of a stylistic technique based on decor and representation.

The schematic web of the historicist epoch, which was based on the late Renaissance, arose out of the need to counter the classicist model with something else. In the 1830s, the architecture of the neo-Renaissance represented this antithesis, and thus historicism began its triumphant march through the cities of Europe. By 'harking back' to this Renaissance-era web, historicism developed a practice that made it easy to 'upload' elements of every style onto a facade. As a result, we find the same web not only in a purely classicist style but also in the national or national-romantic styles of eclecticism.

So what was the weakness of historicism? There were several, but ultimately perhaps only three: the excessive degree of erudition; the inflation of detail; and the complete de facto break with construction, which was rapidly developing in an architecturally and spatially exciting manner.

Let us begin with the extraordinary degree of erudition mentioned above. To master this professorial style of historicism (or a collection of styles based on the neo-Renaissance) required a major effort, involving far more than an architect simply understanding its idiosyncrasies and unique qualities. It led to a situation where he had to learn a colossal volume of material by heart. Despite the outward variety that it produced, it did not, as was later to become apparent, yield any development: historicism scarcely evolved and its only progressive effect was to make historical styles more familiar. The extraordinary role of philological knowledge about the styles of the past was bound eventually to evoke protest.

The architects were up in arms at the difficulties posed by this museological, academic approach, demanding 'simplicity and truth' and personal freedom from historicism. They viewed historicism as an overly complicated intellectual creation and as indiscriminately multifaceted compared with the more uniform and more austere classicism. These demands became ever louder as the nineteenth century drew to a close.

With respect to the inflation of detail, we can say that this process had begun earlier, during the classicist period, but in historicism it became particularly marked. The historicist repetition of detail, the increasing number of buildings and their growing size, and the fact that this style gradually came to embrace all types of building eliminated the centuries-long convention of drawing a clear distinction between the traditionally more ambitious iconic buildings and the less sophisticated everyday buildings. The outstanding works, some 30 per cent of the built environment, and the large number of more mundane buildings began to merge with one another in an ensemble in a rather awkward way, the tendency being for the 30 per cent to forfeit a degree of autonomy. Thus, the harmony of analogy between the outstanding and the mundane seemed to lose its necessary hierarchy in favour of a more uniform style. Historicism embraced not only palaces and churches, stock exchanges and railway stations but also tenement buildings, warehouses, restaurants, jetties, and arsenals. This broad spectrum left no room for individual masterpieces to stand out as significant in the architectural hierarchy. This aberration meant that the details from mundane buildings found their way into the magnificent and extravagantly constructed exceptional buildings. Thus, the Paris tenements of the Haussmann period and the residential and administrative buildings of the Wiener Ring in Vienna still exhibit a masterly architectural plasticity, albeit one reduced to mediocrity. One way to combat this marked mediocrity was to further accentuate the contrast between architectural icons and their surroundings, highlighting either their simplicity or their unique character. At this point, we can clearly see the committed attempt to point up the dwindling difference between the minority 30 per cent of iconic buildings and the remaining 70 per cent that made up the urban environment.

Finally, let us discuss the relinquishment of construction. In the historicist period, construction had attained a fundamentally new level for the first time since Roman antiquity and apparently developed a life of its own. Metal girders, thin metal supports, grid structures, and a more widespread and high-profile role for glass were all accompanying features of historicism. Architects made use of all these innovations, albeit in their respective styles of decoration. Hence, architects concentrated their efforts in two areas: one was the shell, which reflected one or another historical style; the other concerned structure, which was somehow regarded as something shameful, and architects thus sought to dress it up – with ornaments, capitals, bases, and consoles. Eventually they realised that the structure would at some point break out of this stylistic guise and become a coherent sculptural object that had been poorly and merely temporarily concealed beneath the decoration. The events that followed showed that this liberation was not without its problems. While the ornamental casing did not collapse all at once, the tension began to rise, especially since the new structures were the outstanding buildings – our 30 per cent, in other words – with which architects had always been more eager to experiment.

Advances in technology and building materials led to an increase in the physical size of buildings. The Opéra in Paris was still regarded as a very large building at the time of construction, while the parliament buildings in London and Budapest seemed to be colossi clad in the neo-Gothic style, as if a garment had been thrown over them. The same could be said of the Paris and London railway stations and the Palace of Justice in Brussels, which mirrored the style of the neo-Renaissance. In clothing the giants, the style itself became gigantic, which provoked either a formal simplification or an exaggerated monumentality.

This process was even more marked in the early skyscrapers in Chicago and New York. While the neo-Romanesque (and

4.6 **Union Square in New York: a typical early twentieth-century skyscraper built in an eclectic style with richly detailed facades**

4.7 Silhouette of Sacré-Coeur in Paris: the basilica is an essential feature of the Montmartre skyline. This panorama dates from the period of transition from eclecticism to art nouveau. Despite the intricate decoration, the ensemble forms a unified whole, mainly because all the houses exhibit a similar density of detail.

later neo-Gothic) style of these buildings certainly seemed appropriate, it was only really recognisable either in close-ups or in very high-resolution long shots. One can't help thinking that this elaborate decoration was rather superfluous, since it would only have been seen properly by passing pigeons, while human viewers would have been able to get no more than a faint impression or else could only see it at entrance level. With the growing size of prominent buildings, it became increasingly clear that objects on this kind of scale no longer had any need to decorate their spectacular forms and structures. It was precisely these iconic buildings that were later to play a key role in ensembles whose harmony was based on strong contrasts. Henceforth, unfortunately, even simple, mundane buildings without any special features apart from an articulation of their facades were likewise called into question. This later led to a loss of the dignified, detailed 'framing' of outstanding objects.

The loss of decoration on certain types of building was at odds with the idea of the architectural order as the eternal harmony of design. If it was not strictly speaking necessary and did not play any role in harmonising the exterior and the volume, then it was no longer eternal and all-embracing, and its sphere of impact was limited, either by size or height. And if something is not sacred, why do we remain so obsessively attached to it? Why do we spend money on decoration that looks good on a relatively small Parthenon but is not particularly effective on a skyscraper? These and similar questions began to be asked with increasing frequency.

Under pressure from the buildings' dimensions, the superficiality of knowledge, and the dream of renewal, the world of eclecticism was bound to collapse. This happened in Brussels and Paris towards the end of the nineteenth century with the birth of a new style, art nouveau or Jugendstil, which spread rapidly through Europe. Historicism did not give up without a fight, however: it continued to hang on for a long time, putting up resistance, and in some places even survived for several more decades.

A few more words on the temptation of the new. Apparently, this temptation has increased over the course of history: the closer we come to the present, the greater the demand for the new, and the more often it is expected. Let us take a brief look at the longevity of the various styles. The antique architectural order can be said to have lasted for twelve centuries (counting from 6th c. BC to 6th c. AD). The Romanesque developed over two centuries (11th–12th c.), while the Gothic had a little more time (2nd half of 12th–15th c.). The Renaissance reigned for one and a half centuries (15th–16th c.), while the baroque lasted somewhat longer – almost two centuries (late 16th–mid-18th c.). Classicism, by contrast, covered a period of less than a hundred years, from the second half of the eighteenth century to the beginning of the nineteenth. Historicism likewise 'lived' for around 60 years.

We see an accelerating development, an ever more rapid succession of styles and tendencies, and we sense a certain impatience, which led to a kaleidoscopic change and degeneration in taste and eventually to the coexistence of styles or even several individual styles in the work of one and the same architect. Like an overextended spring, this development already gives us a premonition of how it would end: with a sudden state of fatigue, a complete renunciation of decoration, a striving to reveal the constructional and functional skeleton of a building – as the only 'honest' foundation, especially in view of the fact that construction had by then attained a wonderfully independent expressiveness in the main iconic public buildings, which was much more powerful than their decoration. This kind of individual expressiveness was, however, lacking in the simple constructions and very pragmatic forms and structures of most of the ordinary buildings that cities have always comprised. The 'honesty' of these buildings – which, after all, make up at least 70 per cent of every city – tends to be rather disenchanting, and if their facades were not adorned with fine details, be it in terms of their ornamentation, structuring, haptic qualities, or the articulation of their walls, then the result was functional buildings that aged badly and had no sustained artistic appeal. We will speak about this development in the following chapters.

Chapter 5

Accelerated Shifts in Style
Art Nouveau and Neoclassicism in the Early Twentieth Century

By the end of the nineteenth century, historicism was clearly no longer new and exciting, even if it still possessed some definite potential for development. Everywhere national styles were evolving, ushering in a new flowering of Romanian, Old Russian, and Germanic-Gothic motifs – or, in the case of the Sacré-Cœur basilica in Paris, regional Romanesque architecture. And yet a certain fatigue was detectable in building methods. Rapid technical and industrial advances and the growing antipathy towards the 'old-fashioned' system of design that went hand in hand with it evidently had repercussions for architectural style. Historicism gradually drifted into something more generalised. Indistinct forms emerged, architects began to adopt a more liberal approach to the faithful reproduction of detail and to distance themselves from the historicist prototype, which ran counter to what historicism had been all about.

This generalised style, freely revisited and retold, was soon followed by a fresh development. The new style was known by many names (art nouveau in Belgium and France, Secession in Austria, Jugendstil in Germany, Modern in Russia, Stile Liberty in Italy) but spoke a consistent language, albeit with many regional dialects, and apparently began as a 'campaign' launched by a small group of architects. In our opinion, however, it would not have managed to establish itself so successfully had it not been for a parallel development that reverberated at every level: the opening of Japan – a country whose culture had until then been completely unknown to Europeans. The introduction to Japanese culture was an absolute revelation, since Japan was one of the few countries that had remained completely untouched by the international classicist trend and had a highly developed culture of its own that was entirely independent of Europe. It was characterised by an extraordinary freedom in the use of ornamentation featuring plant motifs in combination with markedly orthogonal wooden screen grids – for instance, in the Japanese coloured woodcuts with their traditional flower and bird motifs. Collecting Japanese prints became a widespread passion among European intellectuals. We find copies of Hiroshige prints in the paintings of Van Gogh, and the influence of Japanese visual culture is

5.1 **The building of the Liszt Ferenc Academy of Music in Budapest: the main facade is decorated in art nouveau style with sculptures of famous musicians and composers.**

evident in the works of Gauguin, Schiele, Klimt, and Mucha, and naturally extended to the flowing lines of the plant ornamentation used by art nouveau architects. The new forms evolved in several different centres or schools (as had been the case with neoclassicism and historicism), but there were also a number of individual creative figures who approached the language of art nouveau cautiously and almost playfully, taking up new tendencies and impulses that were 'in the air'.

At the beginning of the 1890s, Victor Horta took a decisive step forwards in Belgium, designing a whole series of villas – first and foremost the Hôtel Tassel in Brussels (1892) – that generated a new style based on the natural world, the free line, and a sharp contrast between stone and metal.

The feeling of pulsating volume was doubtless what was new about art nouveau and what distinguished it from historicism. Despite quoting the baroque, the latter had never succeeded in breathing so much life into the dead form. Even by baroque standards, the new style enjoyed far more freedom: if asymmetry had still been unthinkable in the baroque, in art nouveau, which combined baroque traditions with discoveries from what until then had been unknown worlds, it became not only possible but something to be aspired to. It is precisely this tendency that we regard as borrowed from Japanese culture, which, unlike Roman antiquity, was not constrained by any demand for symmetry. Thus, because the baroque had been wholly indebted to Roman culture, it was not until the emergence of art nouveau that symmetry could be renounced.

Nevertheless, it is fundamentally striking that a more regulated style repeatedly alternated with one that was new, more emotional, and a great deal freer. For all the differences and the imprecise nature of the comparison, the pairs of styles that displayed this alternating effect can be clearly determined: antique – Gothic; Renaissance – baroque; historicism – art nouveau.

The new style can thus be regarded as the obverse of historicism: it renounced symmetry, detailing, and regular lines and instead embraced painterly chaos and favoured free, curving, capricious lines. It liberated metal from the hidden, disguised role that it had played in historicism since Henri Labrouste. Metal now became ornamental in its own right: the extremely fragile supports and delicate arches that had seemed so naive when eclecticism used them as historicist forms now spoke the new language of intense animation and bionic drama with a profound seriousness.

As mentioned above, the new style was connected with the discovery of new lands. Unlike when Europe tapped the riches of its new colonies (bringing rare colonial objects to European capitals for the purpose of play and study and integrating them into the unchanged imperial system as striking curiosities), here an exchange of cultural traditions between equals became possible, whereby freshly discovered cultural elements exerted a strong appeal, sometimes even acquiring cult status, and new tendencies developed.

Art nouveau emerged at the point when the Europeans recognised that architecture not only existed outside Europe but was actively developing in many parts of the world and producing paradigms that were highly original in terms of both decoration and typology. Outstanding achievements of this kind had often suffered barbaric destruction in the early phases of history – the culture of the Maya and the Aztecs on the territory that is now Mexico being a case in point. Yet since the late nineteenth century, South American architectural motifs – stepped pyramids with decorative friezes – had started to be widely used, as had elements of Arab, African, and, once again, Egyptian architecture.

But the emergence and development of the new style was influenced most of all by the forms and the spirit of cultures from the Far East, namely China and, in particular, Japan. As already mentioned, the latter gave a very powerful impetus to the creative rethinking of all branches of European culture.

5.2 **The Hôtel Tassel by Victor Horta in Brussels impressed contemporaries, who were especially struck by the details of the facade. Although we still find the architecture remarkable today, it no longer forms such a strong contrast to its urban surroundings.**

5.3 Teotihuacán – the City of the Gods: the decorative details on the steps inspired many projects and buildings.

The influence of Japanese culture was particularly evident in the work of artists as different as Whistler, Matisse, and Frank Lloyd Wright. And, of course, art nouveau, with its free treatment of plant ornamentation, and its successor, art deco, with its orthogonal ornamental structures, would have been unthinkable without the decorative and tectonic characteristics of Japanese architecture.

After Horta, the new style was further refined by Hector Guimard in Paris, Henry van de Velde in Brussels, and by Otto Wagner, Joseph Maria Olbrich, and Josef Hoffmann in Vienna. In Moscow, art nouveau experienced a golden age with Lev Kekushev's and Franz (Fyodor) Schekhtel's designs for villas for industrialists, which formally followed the discoveries of Belgian, French, and Austrian architects, often outdoing these models in terms of size or decorative splendour. In Saint Petersburg, several architects, among them Fyodor Lidval, Allan Carl Schulman, and Alexei Bubyr, worked in the Nordic variant of art nouveau with its characteristically rough stone facades and narrow trapezoidal windows. In Great Britain, Charles Rennie Mackintosh developed his own, very restrained dialect, while in Barcelona Antoni Gaudí gave such free rein to his formal language that it attained an almost bionic freedom. In all the centres mentioned, the new style of architecture was accompanied by literary symbolism, which nurtured this style but simultaneously threatened its existence.

5.4 The Baron von Besser tenement house – the only building by the Finnish architect
Allan Carl Schulman in Saint
Petersburg – is a characteristic example of Nordic art
nouveau. The drawing dates
from the year 1998, before
the historic building was
converted in 2002–3 into a
seven-storey hotel and
shopping centre. (left)

5.5 An imaginative rendering
of the Nordic art nouveau
building in Saint Petersburg
(right)

This threat was rooted in the notion that architectural language really ought to be eternal and in a corresponding scepticism about the durability of the new forms. The fear was that these forms and the style itself were far too distinctive and would therefore remain transient. They were thoroughly in keeping with the lifestyle of the bohemian world, perhaps also that of artists and the intellectually curious, and possibly that of the experimentally inclined bourgeois. Yet these categories accounted for only part of the elite, for its younger segment. What were its older or more conservative members to do: seek pragmatism in the now passé historicism? And what about the bankers, who couldn't bring themselves to house their banks in these new-fangled buildings, whose lack of any trace of seriousness in their symbols, sweeping lines, and spirit of decadence created an effect that might be playful, melodramatic at times, or even frivolous? The style might be appropriate enough for boutiques and cafés, but not to convey the monumentality of political power or of banks, museums, and theatres.

A style instilled with the spirit of bohemianism, with a taste of both the exotic and the erotic remained alien not only to the respectable bourgeoisie and aristocracy at the court, but also to part of the artistic elite. It was not long before this segment of the intellectual community began to call for a halt to the visual excesses. Take, for example, Van de Velde's essay *Déblaiement d'art* (Clearing Out Art, 1894) and his subsequent writings, in which he intimated that, in view of the technical advancements, one ought to begin creating buildings and art oneself (*Allgemeine Bemerkungen zu einer Synthese der Kunst* [General Remarks on a Synthesis of Art], 1895 and Was ich will [What I Want], 1901). Reading between the lines, one can already sense the birth of non-decorative architecture! Somewhat later the same author wrote, 'This is the moment that our mission to free the everyday objects around us from these ornaments is revealed, ornaments which have no meaning, no inherent raison d'être, and hence no beauty' (*Die Renaissance im modernen Kunstgewerbe* [The Renaissance in Modern Decorative Arts], 1901).

This idea of liberation from excess soon led to a wish to simplify art nouveau in formal terms too. The style did not only provoke opposition through its exuberance, its symbolism, and its apparent lack of taste; its opponents also took exception to the fact that it was only one of several decorative styles, albeit one of the most successful. Its unmistakeable motifs could easily be reproduced: as designs for ship's decks and for posters, in display windows, on the balustrades of country houses, in the iron girders of metro entrances – everywhere, in other words. The decorative now became the focus of negative attention – initially among architects themselves, because it seemed as if this style was deliberately hiding something, namely the fundamental simplicity and honesty that everyone longed for. It appeared as if it would be sufficient to free it once and for all from its 'deceptive clothing', at which point truth and substance would emerge, perfect simplicity untouched by all the vagaries of fashion.

In his famous essay *Ornament und Verbrechen* (Ornament and Crime, 1908) Adolf Loos proposed a new principle: 'The evolution of culture is synonymous with the removal of ornament from objects of daily use.' Naturally it was to disappear not only 'from objects of daily use' but from architecture as well – as Loos indeed went on to demand in his essay *Architektur* (Architecture, 1910), in which he wrote, 'But the man of our day who, in response to an inner urge, smears the walls with erotic symbols is a criminal or a degenerate.' Freely interpreted, this sentence might become the motto 'Ornament as crime'.

From today's perspective we know that these words led to the liberation of architecture from any kind of 'rigging', in the same way that ships were derigged when steam replaced sail. With this technical metaphor we might bring the history of the alliance between the structural skeleton and its decorative casing to a close, were it not incumbent upon us to describe one more style that made a brief appearance in architecture before and during the revolution.

The art nouveau period was very short. In the capitals of culture it lasted a maximum of ten years. It was succeeded in the years after 1900 by a rather more sober variant, early rationalism, which could be found in the work of Adolf Loos, Hans Poelzig, Peter Behrens, Tony Garnier, and Henry van de Velde. This rational version of art nouveau can be regarded as a prologue to the rationalism that was to come and indeed to modernism in general. However, in the brief period between

5.7 The German Embassy in Saint Petersburg, built between 1911 and 1913 to a design by Peter Behrens: a section of the facade with its monumental architectural order.

1907 and 1914, neoclassicism also had an important role to play. This style, quite obviously a further counterpart to art nouveau, was even more short-lived than its predecessor, lasting only about eight years, although it was no less heroic than art nouveau. In the process of liberating itself from the capricious forms that sought to be 'original at any price', neo-classicism developed its own programme of liberation, but in this case liberation from the tastelessness of eclecticism and art nouveau and, even more importantly, from classicism as a misunderstood, dry, and academic style of straight lines. The neoclassical decorative style reintroduced regularity and symmetry together with the antique system of anthropomor-phic proportions. This was supposed to rescue architecture from the storm of industrial aesthetics, from the arbitrary volubility of eclecticism and from art nouveau, of which peo-ple were rapidly beginning to tire. Nevertheless, neoclassi-cist buildings were overshadowed by the precursors to ration-alism and the modernist movement, which was gathering increasing strength; indeed, the manifestos of the neoclassi-cists were simply tacitly ignored by the modernists. This is why a great many architecture aficionados knew very little about the neoclassicism of the early twentieth century, which, amidst the first stirrings of modernism, supplied its own answer to the triumph and decline of art nouveau.

The uncontested leader of neoclassicism in Paris was Auguste Perret, who 'hung' neoclassical bas-reliefs and friezes on a very modern concrete grid frame – such as in the Théâtre des Champs-Élysées. In Germany, Peter Behrens progressed from the proto-rationalism of his famous AEG factory in Berlin (1908/9) to the martial neoclassicism of the German embassy in Saint Petersburg (1912) with its well-proportioned, almost abstract row of half-columns in cold pink granite. The villa Behrens constructed for the archaeologist Theodor Wiegand on the outskirts of Berlin (1911–12) was an example both of how generalised classical architecture had become and of a kind of 'back to the roots' movement – which sought to return to the architecture of ancient Greece. In the works of Oskar Kaufmann we can likewise observe a transition to neoclassi-cism. In Berlin, Kaufmann first built the symbolist Hebbel theatre and subsequently the monumental Volksbühne (1913–14) with its heavy, abstract colonnades. Heinrich Tessenow designed the festival theatre in Hellerau, near Dresden (1911–12), which originally housed the Dalcroze Bildungsanstalt für Musik und Rhythmus (School of Music and Rhythm). Here Tessenow created a generalised archaic symbol in the form of an antique temple as a sacred place of art.

In Vienna, Adolf Loos designed the facade of the fashion shop Goldman & Salatsch (completed in 1911) as an almost 'naked' abstraction and added a row of Doric columns, which were clearly suited to this abstraction. Loos seems to have been an opponent of wall decoration of any kind, yet for the cladding of the first two floors he used the highly intricate natural vein-ing of the marble slabs, whose rich pattern formed a wonder-ful contrast to the windows of the 'house without eyebrows', as his contemporaries called it, as well as to the minimalist fronts of the upper floors, which pedestrians could not see close up. Also in Vienna, Josef Hoffmann, built a villa (1913–15) in the neoclassical style for the banker Otto Primavesi. Strange, ahistorical, abstract forms testify to an intensive search for the classical in the present. Hoffmann had the walls of the villa's halls clad from top to bottom with wooden panels, each panel decorated with asymmetrical plant orna-ments, which forged a bridge from art nouveau via abstract neoclassicism to art deco, whose time was still to come.

In Switzerland, Charles-Édouard Jeanneret alias Le Corbusier built the Villa Favre-Jacot in Le Locle (1912), abiding to the spirit and letter of neoclassicism.

Finally, in Russia, a whole group of architects strove to create a new architecture that evinced less stylistic generalisation and was even less experimental but drew nourishment, more than in the West, from an admiration for the beauty and the 'cultural legacy' of classicism. The result was the new 'eloquent' style achieved by Ivan Fomin, which sought to give expression on a facade to the gentle subtlety of the colonnades of the country manor houses of times long past and to a rough, chthonic, natural vitality. Many Petersburg architects (Vladimir Shchuko, Andrei Belogrud, and Marian Peretyatkovich) worked with the neo-Renaissance style. Here modernism once again clad itself in old garments, with a brutal note, simultaneously heroic and tragic. In Moscow, Ivan Zholtovsky went a step further, using not so much Renaissance style as Renaissance materials: Andrea Palladio's best works experienced a real revival on Russian soil in the form of copies.

For economic or other reasons, some countries never experienced the advent of neoclassicism. In those places neoclassicism was 'delayed' and bore its first, highly significant fruits in the 1920s. Thus, the enormous police headquarters building in Copenhagen, which was 'purely' classical in its architecture, was built by the architects Hack Kampmann (until 1920), Hans Jørgen Kampmann, Holger Jacobsen, and Aage Rafn during the years 1918–24. In Stockholm, Gunnar Asplund created a stylistically generalised vision of timeless classicism in his municipal library (1920–28). The initial impression is of a building that is no longer neoclassicist but rather one in the process of transitioning to contemporary architecture in its pure form. But then the eye takes in the decoration of the huge portals, the ornamental frieze, the stylistically generalised cornice – and suddenly one understands what this is all about: an abstraction with elements of stylisation. In Soviet Russia, the Leningrad School continued the work of neoclassicism in its rough, generalised form, or as Ivan Fomin and his colleagues and pupils from the Academy of Arts – Shchuko, Belogrud, Vladimir Gelfreykh, Noi Trotsky, and Lev Rudnev – called it, 'red revolutionary Doric' (after the ancient Doric order).

In Leningrad, this direction was deliberately cultivated as an antithesis to the modernism and constructivism that dominated during the 1920s and ruthlessly ousted these styles as soon as political circumstances allowed: this formed the basis for the emergence in the early 1930s of Stalinist neoclassicism with elements of art deco.

5.8 **The Émile Jaques-Dalcroze Bildungsanstalt für Musik und Rhythmus (School of Music and Rhythm) – now the festival theatre – was built in 1911 in Hellerau, the famous garden city near Dresden, in accordance with Heinrich Tessenow's designs. The architecture of the main building is characterised by rigorous lines and a noble simplicity. Six tall rectangular pylons support the pediment bearing the school's emblem – the symbol of equilibrium.**

5.9 **Ivan Fomin's Dynamo Club in Moscow was built in the 1930s, but it mirrors the principles of the somewhat earlier 'Red Doric': the uprights of the pillars, which have no capitals, support the plain monumental 'entablature' floor.**

The reason why we have dwelled so long on early twentieth-century neoclassicism is because this style was a response to art nouveau: it combated the irregular and capricious sides of art nouveau, as well as its organic and bionic aspects, and countered them with regularity and symmetry. And it did this at a time when it was already in decline itself and stood almost at the verge of oblivion. Thus, we can discern a tragic element, both in the experiments of the western European architects with their philosophically abstract volumes and in the more direct stylisation of the Russians. Both directions were destroyed by World War I. After that, the picture changed radically in most countries.

Technological progress and the gradual discovery of foreign civilisations by the West accelerated the tempo of architectural development. The process of one style following another was like a stretched spring, which must eventually break as a result of tension and fatigue. One style replaced another with increasing speed, until the most varied kaleidoscope of stylistic decoration flashed past one's eyes, as if seen from a passing express train. The ever tauter line of development was bound to snap. And at the moment when it did, Le Corbusier, the Bauhaus, and constructivism stepped onto the stage of world architecture.

But before we move on to consider the new architecture, we would like to relate how this acceleration affected the urban landscape, everyday life, and objects of everyday use. The rapid pace of change, happening almost in the twinkling of an eye, meant that whole countries got left behind – a long way behind. Sometimes a style that was already long established in France or Germany, for example, did not arrive in another country until half a century later. And it took even longer for a style to reach the colonies. However, once it had arrived in the provinces of Europe or in Latin America, it then became the dominant style, penetrating even the most far-flung corners; it was to be seen in the crests, even the door handles, of every hotel. This is exemplified by the history of classicism in the eighteenth and nineteenth centuries, and the influence of historicism manifested in a similar way.

Art nouveau, too, had been on the point of becoming a universal style, but only in certain parts of Europe, in Russia, and in Japan. The full-blown version never reached the United States, and in Italy there was little to be seen of it, not even in Rome, where it was completely absent. In the early twentieth century, the 'reclothing' of a city or its houses in the new style simply happened too slowly to keep pace with the ever more rapid changes in architectural fashion.

The tendency of styles to flash past at tremendous speed provided an additional argument for the abolition of decorative styles per se, in favour of an attempt once again to create something timeless and unchanging, as had been the practice in antiquity. For, prior to that, a style had always permeated all areas of life, even the most private and the most hidden, and this was proof that it was universally valid and 'right'. Now, however, styles began to make small 'hops' and were so short-lived that they did not even manage to leave behind much in the way of traces. They existed only in the projects of leading architects and the members of the elite who commissioned them. They were therefore regarded as temporary whims of fashion and not as sustained artistic phenomena to be taken seriously. The culture of the time (and it is no different today) thrived on the fact that a broad circle of educated and interested observers, while perhaps not entirely understanding it, were at least willing to enter into dialogue with it. Hence, the search moved away from short-lived fashions in the direction of abstract detailing and the simplification that inevitably went with it. This was not only determined by economic conditions but also motivated by the wish to plan and build something that would be generally valid, something that would gain entry to every house and every room and be comprehensible to any observer receptive to architecture and culture. Art nouveau was unsuitable for this purpose, since by that time it had already been exhausted as a stylistic trend. Nor could it be simplified, because rich decoration was an indispensable part of it.

Neoclassicism, generalised almost to the point of abstraction, did not fit either, since this generalisation gave it a more primitive appearance than its more mature predecessors. There was a great temptation to tear off even the last shreds of antique forms and leave behind just the 'naked' volumes. These strong desires had already materialised in stone, iron, and concrete (in the work of Loos and in certain factory buildings), initially, however, merely in isolated cases. Only subsequent generations of architects and critics took note of and registered these buildings as pioneers of a new epoch, of a revolution in architecture.

In 1914, 3,000 years of ornamentation stood on the brink of annihilation. But at that point no one could have suspected just how profound the changes would be that, as we now know, were just around the corner. Europe plunged into World War I, taking the whole world with it, and the conflict put an end to the idealism of the nineteenth century. It is possible that the decorative element of architecture appeared to be an aspect of old-fashioned idealism too. At any rate, the war marked the beginning of its destruction and annihilation.

Chapter 6
The Architectural Revolution

From a present-day perspective it might seem as if the liberation of architecture from figurative and decorative design could have begun at any time, for the relationship between ornamentation and a building's tectonics and load-bearing structures has always been rather provisional. However, in the context of historical architecture, to speak of an honest construction without ornamentation would be in some small way akin to describing an unpainted canvas as 'honest'. By the beginning of the twentieth century, architecture had been producing variants of the same classicist motifs for over 200 years, and apparently the world of aesthetic culture had had enough of this monotony. But when this old decorative language was finally consigned to the ash heap of history, the baby was thrown out with the bathwater – as is, unfortunately, so often the case – and architecture lost its tactile, sensual basis: its ornamentation, which had been declared 'fundamentally rotten'. Art nouveau, then in its final phases, and in particular art deco, which we shall discuss in detail later, could do nothing to save architecture's figurative and decorative foundation, for although the development of these styles ran parallel to that of the avant-garde, they had a great deal less of the thrilling, regenerative energy that the avant-garde used to negate the past.

What we are dealing with here is an architectural revolution. There is a common tendency to see this as part and parcel of the social revolution, but this is only true of Soviet Russia, and even then only to a limited extent. Even if architects in the rest of the world had links to socialism, or were at least sympathetic to the cause (like the Bauhaus group or Le Corbusier), this connection often tended to be of a more romantic nature. Nonetheless, it was a revolution that came in the form of a cultural explosion, from which the new architecture was born. This revolution rejected most of what was tried and true. It negated the architectural order of antiquity and ornamentation as a fundamental structure for ordering the facade. 'Truth' or 'truthfulness' was the new ideal, and all forms of decoration fell into the category of lies. Architectural order, ornamentation, and embellishment became the enemies of the new form of architecture, which meant that this architecture was not so much founded upon the new notion of truthfulness, but on negation. The emotional energy of negation, as is the case in every revolution, radicalised both discourse and action. As a result, numerous cultural achievements were eradicated, as the past was forcibly swept away by the power of negation. This was the fundamental nature of the architectural revolution.

It began ... well, when exactly did it begin? Perhaps it was in 1914 with Le Corbusier's first drawings for the reinforced concrete frame for his Dom-Ino House, perhaps in the drawings of Antonio Sant'Elia (1912–14), or even with the Fagus Factory designed by Walter Gropius, which was built in 1911. At any rate, it was certainly before World War I. After the war, this architectural revolution was rekindled and spread to encompass an increasing number of countries and cultural metropolises.

What were the main tenets of the new architecture? First and foremost it was, as described above, an architecture of negation, which is why it negated older traditions, and, even more vehemently, the recent past, and why the designs and motifs were not taken from historical sources but were developed from this break with tradition. Any move towards a motif from the past (a temple, palace, or colonnade) meant that the architect had yet to break with tradition, that he still secretly 'clung' to the past. This polarisation lead to a bitter struggle that left no room for negotiation or compromise. The old was to be destroyed – if not physically, then at least in the work of planning and construction. Breaking with tradition was of the utmost importance. Compromisers were to be exposed and condemned.

The new architecture had to be based on truth. Truth was and would be understood as the absence of everything that was not directly necessary for the structure and function of a building and was thus superfluous. The contradiction to all of cultural history inherent to this development was glaringly obvious, for architecture had always been the art of erecting well-proportioned and beautifully decorated buildings, particularly in those instances in which the structure, form, and function of the building were not artistically interesting in and of themselves but instead were rather plain and pragmatic in nature. And we maintain that these represented a 70 per cent majority of all buildings. The demand for functional and structural truth seemed to imply that architecture as art, which, since its inception, had been a foil for the pragmatism of construction and technology, was now redundant, for these pragmatic requirements knew nothing of the search for beauty. If this were true, then after everything that was architecturally superfluous had been removed, only technology, functionality and the dictates of reason would remain. Indeed, the new architecture was in part the architecture of technology, and it would soon become the architecture of a romanticised belief in technological progress that made use of fundamentally new forms. Platonic ideals of pure abstract forms were taken up into the overall view of the new architecture, but the new architecture expressed itself in forms and volumes which, when combined differently, were often remote from structural and functional necessity. These combinations of 'objects' were, ultimately, architecture – and once again, as paradoxical as it might sound, they were deemed superfluous from the pragmatic perspective.

Truth – no longer function (for function would also exist in simpler structures) but the unadorned forms themselves – was reflected in these 'pure' volumes and in exquisite designs. The contrasting of compound volumes developed into one of the leitmotifs and core procedures in the new architecture. At the same time, it also had an intrinsic symbolic significance, as it was used to counter the memory of historical combinations of volumes in the architecture of the past. Such negative memories were the basis for many of the compositional 'traits' of the new asymmetrical and dynamic architecture, which dispensed with adornment and any connection to classical models.

But let us return to architecture's foundations, or, rather, to the shift in these foundations. The architecture of antiquity, as well as all subsequent styles of architecture that took up the traditions of antiquity, was based not only on decoration but on the proportions of the human body, which were ordered in a particular fashion. This ordering could be seen most of all in a building's proportional arrangement and in the appearance of the column: its base, its 'head' (the capital), and its 'body' with all its curves. This articulation, the forms, and the anthropomorphic proportions gave the viewer a sense of affinity with architecture. If we remove the 'head' and the base of the column as well as the entasis – the convexity in the column – then only a post remains, something much simpler and, in a way, abstract. That was the goal of the new architecture: simplicity and abstraction, which were placed on the same level as 'truthfulness', and the independence of the whole from decorative design as a means of articulation.

One might ask if the new architecture is an architecture of disorder or of order. The answer is that it is certainly one of order, but the new order, of course. This new order was also based on new laws of its own. For example, in their attempt to combat historical architecture, its proponents began to negate the idea of symmetry. In the past, overly long facades were broken up by means of symmetrical avant-corps organised around a central axis, thus visually foreshortening the facade. This symmetry was now rejected, as was the subdivision of the static volume into smaller parts. The negation always contained a suggestion of what it was the champions of the new architecture were fighting against.

Nowadays, the architecture of the new order is what we have before us – in terms of both ground plan and volumes. This new order did without the old anthropomorphic proportions and replaced them with abstract ('pure') motifs or motifs derived from technology. Technological advances, which offered so many new possibilities, formed the basis for many of the new architecture's techniques and formal solutions. This did not just apply to the detailing, to open metal joints or technologised forms (such as rivets, joists, or arched girders). The order itself had become technical and thus more mechanistic. The anthropomorphic proportions and rhythm were replaced with mechanistic or technical proportions with endlessly repeating components of the same dimensions or varying progressively in size. Accordingly, the new rhythm was as mechanical and monotonous as that of a large construction site in the age of industrialisation.

Symmetry was also done away with. An architect who sought out compromises or bowed to the pressures of the powerful and opted for a symmetrical ground plan or facade – after all, the tastes of the ruling class did not change, regardless of all the discoveries of the avant-garde – was considered no friend of progress. Symmetry was synonymous with the past and the outdated. The new architecture, on the other hand, strove towards dynamic compositions: acute angles, diagonal arrangements, and innovative combinations of volumes. It also sought out new means of illusion, which, surprisingly, did not accentuate the construction but instead attempted to repudiate it: a glazed corner with a pillar pushed inwards; horizontal bands of windows that hid the supports or parts of a load-bearing wall; thin, deliberately dematerialised pillars on the ground floor that gave massive volumes the appearance of floating in the air instead of visibly shoring them up.

Technology and abstraction replaced the human proportions of the detailing and the figurative qualities that went with this. There was no longer a place for ornamentation in this system. Embellishments were still used in textiles and other forms of 'applied' art, but when it came to the new architecture, such decorations were 'criminal', as Loos described them in the essay referred to earlier. In truth, a 'passion for technology' was supposed to transform architecture into a kind of aestheticised engineering, but the new building material, concrete – an advancement on the old Roman concrete – allowed, or even forced, architects to keep to the architectural laws of the past in the case of certain buildings. These laws were intuitively derived from the laws of gravity and had nothing in common with the new architectural motifs of the floating airships of the future.

All manner of things were done away with! First and foremost, the classical order, the proportional arrangement of the building's facade (its 'face'), and, indeed, the category of the facade itself. This happened at the same time as the gradual 'eradication' of figuration in art in general that manifested itself in the rejection of depictions of reality (that is to say, the non-abstract reality) and the human figure in particular. Accordingly, the visual arts and architecture both underwent similar processes: painting felt that it had exhausted the limits of realism, while architecture continued to distance itself from the past. In architecture, it felt as if the figurative element – also a kind of realism – had been exhausted. In poetry, first the rhyme was abolished, as it, too, had been exhausted, and then the metre. To a certain extent one can also view rhyme as a kind of decoration, a conclusion to a part of the whole like a column's capital, while the rigid metre offers a form of classical order as a decorative organisational system.

All these forms now belonged to the past. After World War I, the Italian futurists, in particular Sant'Elia, found a trenchant angle from which to view innovative architecture, taking an oblique look from below. They created an illusion of movement, a mechanistic acuity in the rhythm of the new architecture. At first this was only on paper, but then new ideas and techniques began to be applied to constructed buildings. And here it emerged that the priorities, as had always been the case with the avant-garde (and this new architecture was most certainly avant-garde), had shifted for the most part. Often this had nothing to do with pre-eminence in quality or significance, but with the priorities involved in devising a technique. As the architecture of the past had basically been 'forgotten' overnight, we do not see a rigorous eradication of the old but rather an almost simultaneous constituting of the new.

Mayakovsky, the best-known poet of the Russian Revolution, once said, 'Poetry is a journey into the unknown.' This was the thinking and metaphorical conceit of an avant-garde poet, and it holds just as true for the architecture of the avant-garde.

The history of the new architecture's conquering of the world has been written many times, and yet it is our opinion that it has never really been written – not even a rudimentary account of it. This assertion can be based on the fact that it is very difficult to establish the precedence of a single master or a single group. We do not claim to present a complete account of the story, nor do we seek to chronicle how the avant-garde's cluster of ideas was uncoiled (or how the tension that had built up in its development dispersed). We shall only stop to examine the stages in its evolution that we believe are important for this book.

In France Le Corbusier discovered new forms. It would even appear that this architectural genius developed and created all of the forms and techniques on his own. His five principles of the new architecture formed the basic programme of its further development. They are as follows: *Open floor plan* – Previously floor plans had been constrained by massive rows of columns or walls; in other words, they were not free. The span widths offered by modern construction techniques allowed for fewer and lighter supporting elements, meaning the space could be opened up to enable new functions.

Unadorned, functional, and in some instances non-load-bearing exterior walls – Previously the facade had been an indispensable decorative part of the load-bearing exterior wall, but now it was no longer required in construction, meaning it could be independent in terms of material and form.

Visible pillars, particularly in the open ground-floor space – This ended the visual principle of lighter upper floors and a heavy base, which was more in line with the laws of physics. Instead, they created an illusion of floating and made it possible to create a public space on the ground floor, which was now largely freed from structural requirements.

Ribbon windows – These were an additional illusory device that allowed for brighter rooms: supposedly less light was allowed through the individual vertically aligned punch windows of the past.

Flat roof – Such roofs allowed for roof terraces, a living space which is more important in warmer climates. It was polemically set against the gable roof of the past, which is better suited for protecting buildings from rain and snow in colder climates.

6.1 **Le Corbusier's only building in Moscow, the Tsentrosoyuz Building. Here we can see the dynamic form as well as the floating volume and radical ribbon windows.**

Le Corbusier realised this programme in a dozen villas and a handful of larger buildings. The new architecture found its physical incarnation. It became material.

In the Netherlands, the De Stijl group constructed buildings using the new forms. Theirs was a unique version of the new that had more to do with the formal rhythm found in painting and with Mondrian's compositions. The results were impressive and noteworthy, for the group had succeeded in transforming the geometrical abstraction found in painting into architectural volumes. And their appearance was different from that of the buildings appearing in Prague, for example, where the principles of cubism were being manifested in architecture at around the same time. In the Weimar Republic, the innovative impulse split into two currents after the war.

6.2 **Kurt Bärbig's meat processing plant in Dresden (1930) draws upon
Erich Mendelsohn's expressionist aesthetics and sculptural approach.**

On the one hand, there was Erich Mendelsohn, who had already put his own expressionist phase behind him. Together with Hans Poelzig and Hermann Finsterlin, he was one of the main representatives of this stylistic direction in the post-war era. Mendelsohn created his own expressionist stylistic variation. It was marked by accentuated rounded corners and metaphorical forms that called to mind movement or even flying. A second German stylistic variation was represented by the Bauhaus, a group of architects, artists, and designers who founded an institute that served as an experimental laboratory. Walter Gropius designed a building for the Bauhaus that embodied the new architecture. This building spoke its own language, a language that was different from that of Le Corbusier: it had more didactic qualities, more emphasis on the details, which sometimes became symbols. This style was taken up some years later by Hans Scharoun, while Bruno Taut represents a rather restrained version of it. Alongside these masters we find Mies van der Rohe, whose uncompromising passion for gestures symbolising technology could be seen in his plans for a skyscraper for Berlin's Friedrichstrasse; however, he was only able to execute his design after he had left Germany and emigrated to the United States.

Finally, the new style would undergo an unusual development in the Soviet Union. This style, usually referred to as constructivism, had three phases: the early phase was largely played out on paper; the middle phase was a period of autonomy and experimentation; and the late phase was one of simultaneous triumph and tragedy.

6.3 **The Rusakov Workers' Club, designed by Konstantin Melnikov. Together with El Lissitzky's designs for horizontal skyscrapers (Wolkenbügel), this building became the prototype for all console-style architectural compositions of the 20th and 21st centuries.**

In the early phase, Italian futurism and German expressionism came together with motifs from the world of technology in the workshops of the state art college Vkhutemas in Moscow (1920–27). Something new arose from this mix that resonated with the experiment of the socialist revolution and with the experiences of Western architects. Furthermore, Soviet architects found themselves confronted with a unique challenge: in 1918 the capital was relocated from Petrograd to Moscow, which at the time was made up primarily of two- and three-storey buildings. A new, radically innovative capital of the communist world was to be created there. Naturally the

project attracted all the talented and staunch avant-garde artists to Moscow, where they founded architecture schools in the hope of educating creators of the new style. Petrograd, later renamed Leningrad, became a breeding ground for the opposition. Proletarian neoclassicists spearheaded the counter-attacks, and in the early 1930s the avant-garde was outlawed.

The middle phase gifted us with a number of buildings, of which the Moscow clubs designed by Konstantin Melnikov and Ilya Golosov are of outstanding importance. These clubs are significant examples of how technology, formal expression, and emotional resurgence worked together in the new style's best buildings in the USSR and led to a few outstanding solutions for design and formal issues: Melnikov's 'speaking machine elements', which gave rise to buildings in the form of gearwheels and other machine components as well as a building shaped like a tractor, or the abstract forms of Golosov (for example, the glass cylinder with its massive belt of beams on the top floor of the Zuev Worker's Club in Moscow). These designs were created independently of those of their colleagues in Europe, which supports the idea that the Russian school was autonomous. This school devised more tangible forms and gave expression to the emotional tenor of the technical revolution instead of subordinating it. At the peak of this development we find iconic sculptural buildings whose volume and form offered daring contrasts to Moscow's old urban structure. As the architects themselves said, 'We come with the new harmony, we bring the harmony of contrasts based on an incisive dialogue with our surroundings.' In this manner, their fundamentally new way of handling the historical past made this past part of their architectural composition, providing it with a deeper perspective and lending it meaning. For his new high-rises in Paris, Le Corbusier suggested that the historical buildings should simply be torn down, as he viewed them as outdated and unusable. The Russian constructivists, however, consciously allowed the two opposing elements – the old and the new – to clash with one another, which led to an essentially new form of dialogue: a dialogue of contrast. This principle, we believe, was soon taken up by architects all around the world. It constitutes both the unique strength and the weakness of modern architecture in the twentieth and twenty-first centuries.

The state experiment of constructing a new society along with its own symbols encouraged the search for an appropriate form of architectural expression. Based on this fundamental idea, constructivism reached Russia in the late 1920s and reached its high point in the early 1930s. Constructivist buildings became conspicuous elements in the redesigned urban landscape. The greatest attention was paid not only to residential buildings with a large number of collective spaces designed for everyday use and social functions but also to public buildings: municipal buildings, train stations, publishing houses, department stores, and workers' clubs. They were generally the result of high-profile competitions that highlighted this contrast and led to a great deal of discussion. In Russia, this phase corresponded with the visionary drawings of Yakov Chernikhov and Ivan Leonidov, who impressively represented the spatial compositions of the new architecture and prompted constructivist architecture to engage in new formal 'turns', new levels of grandiosity, and new polemics against the old, reactionary surroundings.

At this point, there were not many more residential blocks in the new style in the USSR than there were in Germany, but the buildings themselves had another dimension. The new architecture reached into all areas of art, and the mere look of it and the example it set forth influenced theatre productions as well as clothing. It did not always achieve the same degree of detail as the work of the Bauhaus masters, but it did display a fine sense of the novelty and originality inherent to the ideas of the avant-garde and attempted to express these traits. This allowed an outpost of the avant-garde to arise in the Soviet Union, most notably in Moscow, although it also reached extraordinary heights in Yekaterinburg. This pocket of extreme ideas was irresistible to architects, researchers, and architecture aficionados from all over the world. It offered a completely new concept of urban development and aesthetics, which extended to the sharp contrasts evident in the dialogue with the historical surroundings. We would describe this concept as the harmony of contrast as opposed to the harmony of analogy that is so often mentioned.

The world's most famous modern architects, such as Le Corbusier, Hannes Meyer, André Lurçat, and Ernst May moved to Russia in order to work there. Walter Gropius participated in international competitions in the Soviet Union. These architects shared the ideas of the Russian avant-garde and thus can be said to have taken part in this unique phenomenon. Russian architects such as El Lissitzky, for example, actively worked together with the Bauhaus. The result was that the world of the new architecture was unified at the international level.

The new aesthetic found its way into everyday life: furniture, everyday objects, theatre, and film. The new style in architecture and daily life sought to subjugate other styles and, to a certain degree, achieve a kind of totalitarian power. In his villas and residences, Le Corbusier enthusiastically sought out forms that would impress the liberal bourgeoisie or the bohemian milieu. He could only dream that the new aesthetic would influence every area of life to the degree that it did in the Soviet Union for more than ten years. Bauhaus architects constructed residential quarters in Berlin, Hamburg, and Stuttgart as well as villas in the well-to-do suburbs, but during the 1920s they could never have claimed that the new aesthetic was all-pervasive, as was the case in the Soviet Union. This was the most exciting aspect of late Soviet constructivism: it was the materialised dream of the new architecture's universal style.

While this style was actively spreading, a notable development occurred. The architectural avant-garde upset the balance between exceptional buildings and the urban landscape as a whole. The new architecture demanded universal validity and aesthetic uniqueness at the same time – despite the declared precedence of mass housing. It was revolutionary in every aspect, which is why it destroyed the balance between the buildings belonging to the category of iconic, exceptional masterpieces and the urban background with its humane proportions, tiny details, and surfaces that were anthropomorphic and to which human beings could relate. However, this urban backdrop fulfilled an important function in terms of urban planning in that it set up a humble yet worthy frame for unique objects. In a typical historical city, such 'background' architecture made up 70 to 80 per cent of the built environment and thus constituted the overwhelming majority of buildings. Before the beginning of the new era, this architecture was free to be what it was: unknowing, backward, provincial, or even narrow-minded and stuffy. But now this majority found itself under attack, as architects of the triumphant style designed (and built!) entire urban quarters with buildings of the same type with standardised flats filled with standardised furniture.

Here one could make the following objection: did not the Empire style (along with Biedermeier, its 'sub-style' for the middle classes) or historicism display the same degree of stylistic unity? Our answer is yes, there was a tendency towards the universal, but this did not require the renunciation of details and ornament. Such decorative details were traditionally produced by local artists and artisans, but the new aesthetic led to a situation in which these artists and artisans were no longer needed 'for the people' (and drawn, it should be said, from the ranks of the people). The great artists now wanted to do everything themselves, everything that the smaller artists and artisans had done before – they were bent on working for the masses, standardising their own inventions and producing them on the assembly lines. Here we can already see the tendency that would later enter into full force: the utopian impulse of the new architecture and its direct relationship to the forced levelling down of all people and their living environments. The question of whether this equality was real or only desired is not so important in this context.

It is worth noting that this 'unbalancing' encountered strong resistance. The inhabitants of the new buildings desired not only a robust and practical place in which to live but also structures that had an attractively designed appearance. This was the resistance that came 'from below'.

But there was also resistance 'from above'. Where the aristocracy and upper middle classes exerted or even increased their influence, as was the case in the bourgeois democracies, these groups wished to demonstrate their status, wealth, and influence. The new architecture offered no means of doing so (indeed, the only means available was the conscious, but at times shocking, contrast with the historical surroundings). The new villas did represent openness and freedom – but the traditional discreet presentation of status and privilege could not be communicated by the new style. It appears as if the majority of people commissioning the new architecture in the West never learned to utilise the new language as a means of expressing its uniqueness. In places in which the power was in the hands of totalitarian or at least authoritarian forces and where it was perceived as the true instance of government that it indeed was – that is to say where it had sufficient power and authority – such forces wished to express their importance, position, and might in as articulate a manner as possible. Here, too, resistance arose against the new architecture. And as we will see in the next chapter, these powers would become ever stronger in the years to follow.

6.4 **The Zuev Workers' Club in Moscow (1927; architect: Ilya Golosov) is one of the most expressive and well-known examples of constructivism. The building consists of regular geometric forms, evidence of the cubist influences in its design. The centre of the composition is a vertical glass cylinder, which holds the entire volume together. The neighbouring building is a monument of industrial architecture: the Miusskaya tram depot (1874). The result is an example of the harmony of contrast between two fundamentally different principles.**

Chapter 7

A Last Burst of Figuration
Art Deco and Totalitarian Neoclassicism

So many people are interested in this period, and yet it has never managed to find its rightful place in twentieth-century architectural history. Why is this? From the perspective of modern architecture it was a step backwards, a retreat, a defeat, a temporary surrender of avant-garde principles. Furthermore, the final phase of this style was connected with the most brutal dictatorships of the twentieth century and is directly associated with their atrocities.

What did it look like in its early phase? It was different everywhere, and for a variety of reasons. First of all, it is important to emphasise that we are talking about two styles, which at times developed parallel to one another, and at times in succession. Sometimes they were even combined. One retained the pure form but added decoration and ornamentation from various national traditions. This is the so-called art deco. The other returned to the megalithic forms of distilled neoclassicism with its love of exaggeration. This style was actively developed in totalitarian states in particular, where sometimes, for example in the Soviet Union of the Stalinist era, it was combined with art deco elements.

Let us start by looking at art deco. This style had its own geography and chronology, its own set of themes, its own stylistic characteristics and processes. Yet it had no universal character, it was not all-embracing. It lived next door to the avant-garde but never invaded its neighbour's territory, preferring to concede instead. It was ambivalent by nature: playful, yet deeply earnest. It liked to play with allusions: with bionic associations, different folklore traditions, and historical styles. But it was deadly serious about its defining characteristic: art deco was about expensive execution. Superficial opulence was an option, but the hallmarks of genuine wealth were better: gemstones, gold, and other treasures. Affluence was ostentatiously displayed, flaunting the achievements of the bourgeoisie. This predestined the style for later incarnations: even today art deco is the go-to style whenever an open display of wealth is called for.

Art deco was undoubtedly a continuation of the art nouveau style, and it achieved this masterfully, transforming natural forms and historicism alike. It emerged in 1920s' France and Belgium and enjoyed huge successes in both the north and south of the American continent. This style could express itself in interior design, it could inhabit a sculpture, grace facades, and structure the vast volumes of skyscrapers. Two famous high-rises in New York secured its international fame: the Chrysler Building and the Empire State Building.

7.1 **The 44-storey Essex House Hotel in New York is considered a prime example of art deco.**

7.2 **Fifth Avenue on the corner to Central Park: another typical example of New York's art deco 'ziggurat' skyscrapers**

7.3 **The facades on the Avenida Roque Sáenz Peña – one of the main streets in Buenos Aires – have unmistakable elements of neoclassicism and art deco.**

The same stylistic features could be found in the Soviet architecture of the 1930s, when the regime was looking to replace the outlawed constructivism – with something less ascetic, so that the 'dictatorship of the proletariat' could show off its successes in boosting general prosperity. Buildings by Alexey Shchusev and Daniil Fridman and metro stations by Alexey Dushkin and Dmitry Chechulin can also be categorised as art deco, albeit with a few reservations. These relate to the fact that 1930s' Soviet architecture (this applies to Shchusev as well as Vladimir Shchuko and Vladimir Gelfreykh) mostly took its cues from the late art deco of the same decade and in particular from its French and American variations. This later version (the Palais de Tokyo and similar buildings in Paris) entered into an intense dialogue with the architecture of the classical order and carved out a path for itself by adapting and stripping it down.

Art deco seemed content to cede to more monumental styles: in Italy as well as in Stalin's USSR, it was succeeded by totalitarian neoclassicism. In France, in the late 1920s, a branch of art deco attempted to fuse with the architecture of the avant-garde but succeeded only in diluting it. An entire street of villas by the architect Robert Mallet-Stevens skilfully mimicked Le Corbusier's aesthetic, but the curves were more delicate and the balconies more playful than any avant-garde architect could have dreamed of. The same tendency manifested itself in other European countries in the early 1930s: in Belgium, the USSR (for example in the postconstructivism of Ilya Golosov), in Poland, Estonia, Latvia, and Lithuania.

To conclude, one could say that art deco was a reaction to modernism and the banishment of decoration and human proportions from avant-garde architecture. This reaction generally manifested itself in countries with democratic governments (the Soviet Union was an exception, and even there it was only during a brief period in the early 1930s when the totalitarian machine was still under construction). In the direct development of art deco's forms its motifs were sharpened and arranged geometrically. Another line of development, a later variation of art deco known as Streamline Moderne, led to an alliance of avant-garde architecture and the upper-middle-class lifestyle. The love of luxury furnishings and exquisite artistic details remained constant in all its variations. A number of solutions that were arrived at in the 1920s as a means to adapt neoclassical motifs later went on to develop monumental and even brutalist traits, without losing any of their elegance. From a distance of more

than half a century, art deco can be regarded as a 'dolce vita' experiment on the eve of catastrophe, but one that may have lacked the necessary resolve. The opponents of art deco from the modernist and neoclassical camps, which we will come to next, were far more radical in their views and more hostile towards the competition.

In totalitarian states, neoclassical styles were far more determined than art deco. They laid claim to absolutist environmental design, and in some countries, Germany and the USSR in particular, they were applied universally. Totalitarian neoclassicism was invented in Italy, although there were already clear echoes of it in the 'Red Doric' of the Leningrad School in 1920s' Russia and in the archaic neoclassicism of Peter Behrens and Heinrich Tessenow in Germany. Italy also had its own form of rationalism, which was used for building universities (although not the main buildings), sanatoriums, and even fascist party offices. The totalitarian style, however, dominated in each instance. It stemmed from the eclectic Roman fantasies of Armando Brasini and established itself in the work of Marcello Piacentini as a sophisticated and distilled monumental neoclassical system.

The totalitarian Italian style was an abstracted form of neoclassicism. Its rhythm had already become more mechanical, yet the idea of the architectural order and a structural proportioning redolent of classicism is still recognisable in every building. The red-brick walls and travertine details and columns were a direct reference to imperial Rome. The engraved stone inscriptions, the stylistically universalised mosaic images and stone reliefs, the desire for a homogeneous ensemble of buildings devoid of all contrast – all signified their affiliation with a unified style. The subsequent absence of contrasting buildings is a phenomenon that can be found in all strains of totalitarian neoclassicism. All the elements were always part of an ensemble; subordination was strictly observed, and exceptions were inadmissible. This did guarantee a certain quality, albeit one that paled by comparison with the Renaissance or classical standards.

Accordingly, we can see that, under the sway of Piacentini's ideas and forms (which did not enjoy absolute dominance because the rationalists were allowed to exist in parallel), a unified style of ceremonious elegance took shape in Italy. In the 1920s and particularly in the 1930s it developed as neoclassical variations in the residential areas on the outskirts of

Rome. Against this background, the buildings in which the abstraction and formalisation of neoclassical ideas reached their peak were the ones that stood out: the Palazzo del Lavoro, for instance, or the EUR ensemble for the World's Fair in Rome (1938–43; Giovanni Guerrini, Ernesto Bruno La Padula, and Mario Romano). Other typical examples were buildings with an unusually high degree of decoration and sumptuous neoclassical ornamentation in the style of parts of the Foro Mussolini: the Palazzo della Farnesina (Palazzo del Littorio) and the Stadio dei Marmi (Marble Stadium) by Enrico Del Debbio (1927–35).

The relative freedom enjoyed by architecture in fascist Italy was in stark contrast to the truly totalitarian propagation of neoclassicism in Nazi Germany. Here, there were no alternative styles or currents whatsoever after the Bauhaus was shut down in 1933 and avant-garde architects were forced into exile in the United States or Great Britain. The dominant figures in German architecture were Paul Ludwig Troost and Albert Speer. They created a new style which perpetuated the memory of classicism from the first half of the nineteenth century (primarily represented by the work of Leo von Klenze, along with that of Karl Friedrich Schinkel and Ludwig Persius), as well as the neoclassicism of the early twentieth century (its principal proponents being Josef Hoffmann, who taught Troost, and Heinrich Tessenow, who taught Speer).

Classicism was regarded as an immortal, inviolable value, the keystone of world heritage, which ennobled every architectural space and lent historical depth to every building. This was the prevailing conception of classicism and its application in the totalitarian style. But German architects applied classicist practices and motifs sparingly and were more interested in abstracting the classical heritage than developing it. They might install a portico, but with pylons instead of columns: if they used entablature, it would be simplified with an exaggerated and strongly protruding cornice. If they worked with rhythm, it was consciously mechanical and monotonous. Restrained colours, superhuman dimensions, the endless rhythm of windows with simplified dripstones or none at all – these are the key visual elements of this architecture.

The overall appearance was relatively heavy and solid, with no apparent reference to human proportions, and yet it was easily applied to different structural schemes. In residential areas and office buildings it was enhanced with traditional German architectural traits: the gable roof, Gothic framed entrances in clay, arcades, and niche statues. This was the everyday version of the style and it spread across countries east of Germany, where architecture's formal language and devices were taught in a similar way in universities and art schools, thereby giving history a voice in the new architecture.

In the early twentieth century, town houses and suburban villas were built in and around Saint Petersburg and Moscow for the aristocracy and upper middle classes. These buildings, which adopted the style of Russian classicism and various versions of the Renaissance – primarily the Palladian – were designed by Ivan Fomin, Vladimir Shchuko, and Ivan Zholtovsky. Alexey Shchusev was commissioned by the imperial family to develop the neo-Russian style with its vivid interpretations of buildings from the twelfth to the seventeenth century, the time before Peter the Great.

As paradoxical as it might seem, after the 1917 Revolution the Bolsheviks favoured the very architects who had built their reputations working with the Tsars – it may be, of course, that these architects found a way to ingratiate themselves with the Bolsheviks. Fomin, Shchuko, and Zholtovsky continued their neoclassical experiments in the 1920s (albeit forgoing pure neoclassicism in favour of modern forms). Fomin formed a group of disciples of revolutionary neoclassicism drawn from his most talented students at the Petersburg Academy. They had never stopped believing in classical architecture and regarded it as the pinnacle of architectural progress, instilling this respect in their own ranks of students. In the early 1930s, after the first round of the international competition for the Palace of the Soviets in Moscow, which attracted both avant-garde architects (Gropius, Le Corbusier, the Vesnin brothers, and Meyer) and neoclassicists (Brasini and Zholtovsky) from around the world, Stalin turned his back on constructivism in favour of an architecture with more pomp and detail. This was how the neoclassicists once again became the master builders of the state style. Soviet architecture had to be reinvented under Stalin and purged of all traces of modernism. The principle elements were taken from neoclassicism, but without the abstraction typically found in Italy and Germany. The new Soviet style suffered from growing pains and followed a zigzag path to maturity. Initially, it contained many of the rudiments of constructivism (this version was known as postconstructivism), before the dynamic and angular compositions were shed in favour of increasingly

7.4 An architectural fantasy: imaginative rendering of the Palazzo del Lavoro in Rome

7.5 The hypermonumental colonnade of the Haus der Deutschen Kunst in Munich from 1937, designed by Paul Ludwig Troost

regular, symmetric volumes and facades. The 'Red Doric' of the revolution which was closely affiliated with Italian neoclassicism and endorsed by Ivan Fomin (he died prematurely in 1936) was favoured over art deco's eclectic mix of neoclassical forms and elements. The method suggested by Ivan Zholtovsky, a man who consistently eschewed modernism, of reviving and adapting neo-Renaissance compositions for the new dimensions and functions also enjoyed some success. The facade he designed in Moscow's Mokhovaya Street unites extensive office-block glazing with the Corinthian colossal order of the Loggia del Capitaniato. This became the ultimate manifesto for the new style and signed the death warrant for the Soviet avant-garde.

From this point on, residential buildings looked like inflated Florentine palazzi, and sanatoriums and academic institutes were dressed in the facades of Palladian villas. Soviet architects studied the Italian culture of the fifteenth and sixteenth centuries in libraries – some of them had even seen it first hand before the Soviet era – and they used this cultural heritage to create a richly detailed variety of alternatives to the totalitarian neoclassicism of Italy and Germany.

Were totalitarian styles universal? Yes and no. In Italy, neoclassicism was on an almost equal footing with functionalism and rationalism (although it always had precedence). Germany and the USSR banished and banned modernist styles and only those architects who signed up to the totalitarian style were allowed to continue working. In both Germany and the USSR, architecture was entirely dominated by totalitarian neoclassicist styles. Only in the interior design of private rooms and ministerial offices did it become clear that while the neoclassicist style might be ideal for the design of a formal hall, it did not work for a living room or a restaurant, for sofas, lamps, tables, or chairs, nor for that matter could it be applied to the design of machines or ships. For such functional objects and interiors it became customary to use art deco elements. This might seem paradoxical, but only at first. When you think about it, the emotional tenor of neoclassicism sits uncomfortably with private life and other everyday areas – it proved to be too far removed from human dimensions and therefore felt out of place. The relatively simple, 'human' details of art deco offered a more suitable palette for this task. In the USSR, however, attempts were made in the post-war years to design everyday objects and furnishings in other historical styles, for example in the Empire tradition.

Nazism in Germany and fascism in Italy were defeated and disappeared at the end of World War II. The neoclassicist styles, which ever since have been associated with the political regimes under which they flourished, disappeared with them.

In the USSR, neoclassicism continued after the end of the war. One strand (Zholtovsky's school) took up the Italian neo-Renaissance tradition; others tried to fuse neoclassicism, art deco, and even the neo-Russian style (Shchusev's architecture, the skyscrapers of Lev Rudnev, Vladimir Gelfreykh, Michail Minkus, and Leonid Polyakov). Moscow's seven famous towers clearly demonstrate the influence of the New York and Chicago skyscrapers, whose design fuses art deco with elements of the classical architectural order.

Neoclassicism was exported from the Soviet Union to numerous other countries that became 'socialist' after the war. In eastern Europe this included East Germany, Poland, and Romania, and in Asia, Mongolia and China. This architecture became a hallmark of 'real socialist' countries and a way to distinguish between East and West Germany, North and South Vietnam, and North and South Korea.

In our view, not only did the totalitarian styles lay claim to universality (with the exception of the private sphere, and even this was inconsistent), often they actually achieved it. In the USSR under Stalin, an administrative building in a kolkhoz (collective farm), an ammunition depot, a petrol station, and a tram stop were all built in the same style. This style was dictated from above and had a theoretical foundation. Most importantly, the building industry was equipped for this style, and thus every detail was guaranteed to be of a relatively high standard.

Stalin's death in 1953 brought neoclassicism to an almost immediate close in the USSR, although building work on the palaces and high-rises of the Stalin era continued and was carried to completion over the next two and a half years. However, the government decree of 4 November 1955, 'On the Elimination of Excess in Design and Construction', put an end to any decorative elements that would make buildings more expensive.

This event marked the culmination of a period of significant change on the world's architectural map. Following the destruction of the fascist powers and the final reckoning with Stalin's personality cult, attitudes to neoclassical architecture

7.6 **Lenin, from above and below: an imaginative rendering of the Palace of the Soviets and Soviet neoclassical architecture of the 1930s (left)**

7.7 **An imaginative rendering of the art deco locks on Moscow's Volga Canal, decorated in monumental style with Soviet symbols (right)**

7.8 Architect's office: an imaginative rendering of the Soviet architecture of the 1940s and 1950s. It shows the relationship between the Moscow towers and their surroundings as well as the prototype for all Stalinist high-rises: the Palace of the Soviets with the enormous sculpture of Lenin on the top. Legend has it that the plan was for Lenin's head to be big enough to hold a congress hall. Lissitzky's horizontal skyscrapers (Wolkenbügel) float in the air – constructivist ideas were still foremost in the minds of architects during the Stalinist era.

changed, and either the style as a whole or just the element of 'excessive' decoration was regarded as a debased appendage of the political regime that had created it. This is deeply unfair, of course. We do not believe that artworks should be judged according to how democratic or humane the political systems of their time were. The masterpieces of ancient Rome, the Colosseum for example, are not something we associate today with the inhuman spectacles and events that were held there. In the same way, we do not connect medieval or baroque architecture with the history of the Inquisition. But the crimes of totalitarian regimes against their own peoples and those of other countries and the tragic destinies for which they were responsible weighed so heavily that it was impossible to ignore the politics and see them purely in artistic terms. Before the war, many countries regarded neoclassical buildings as a good solution for large-scale public buildings. Take, for example, the National Art Gallery in Washington, built in 1941 according to the designs of a staunch neoclassicist and expert in museum architecture, John Russell Pope. After the war, the view of architecture in the new, free world had to change fundamentally.

The avant-garde masters who had suffered under dictatorships and been forced into exile or banned from practising – Mendelsohn, Mies, Gropius, Scharoun, Melnikov – never abandoned their dream of new forms and a new statement, an architecture of freedom rather than of neoclassical dictates. The world was receptive and amenable to international modernist architecture – the immediate successor to the ideas of the avant-garde.

Before the inception of the avant-garde, ornamentation had played a role in every style and every national tradition. Suddenly, decoration as a part of architecture and of the well-ordered neoclassical system was again banned from architectural language, and every form of ornamentation was associated with the architecture of the criminal regime. Architectural culture was deprived of the opportunity to decorate surfaces, to articulate and vary them, and ultimately make them more human by providing them with the complex relief that allowed the buildings to collect the dust of time, form a patina, and age gracefully.

7.9 **View of Trinity Church, a neo-Gothic building surrounded by typical New York art deco skyscrapers**

Chapter 8

The Triumph of Modernism after World War II, the Short Postmodernist Phase, and Modernism's Resurgence

After World War II the world began to rebuild itself. In Europe and North America, democracy went hand in hand with a commitment to art and modernist architecture. In the postwar climate, it was often radical versions of modernism, so at odds with neoclassical architecture, that seemed to best illustrate democratic political tendencies.

Neoclassicism was discredited through its direct associations with totalitarian regimes. In the early 1950s neoclassical architecture was still being developed in the USSR and the countries in the 'socialist camp'. This became another argument against neoclassicism and against ornamentation and decoration on buildings in general. Everyone could see from the example of the USSR and the socialist countries that a dictatorship (in this case a socialist dictatorship) favoured columns, cornices, pylons, and grandiose facade decoration. Further support for this argument could be found in Spain, where, even after the war, Franco's authoritarian regime continued to build in the style of abstract neoclassicism.

Neoclassicism thus found itself scapegoated: firstly, because of its figuration and decorative design, which was held to be superfluous by the champions of the avant-garde, and secondly, because of its association with dictatorships.

All the forces of the 1920s' avant-garde came to the fore again, after having been compelled to stand in the shadows since the 1930s. In France, it was Le Corbusier, who had never parted ways with his modernist architecture. In Great Britain, Lubetkin's ideas were revived. In West Germany, Hans Scharoun returned from exile and created a new version of the avant-garde. In Italy, the rationalists took over from Marcello Piacentini and Armando Brasini. As we know, the Italian rationalists were never expelled from the country and had continued to work under the fascist regime. Mies and Gropius, who had fled to America before the outbreak of war, built fantastic, expressive buildings demonstrating the beauty and substance of the new architecture: this included the stylish use of glass and metal, and combinations of the two, as well as an elegant embrace of technology in the detailing. They showed how expressive and functional the monumental, mechanical rhythm could be.

It was an inconspicuous but determined modernist revolution that changed the world's architectural landscape: the visions and dreams of the 1920s were realised at a lightning pace. City skylines were defined by flat roofs atop upright and horizontal rectangular buildings. Where once it had been facades, now it was pavements that defined the street lines, while the houses were strung out as dotted lines or series of diagonal dashes. Sometimes half a dozen identical, unadorned rectangular buildings would be grouped together

8.1 **New York skyscrapers: in the background the MetLife Building (until 1981, the PanAm Building), co-designed by Bauhaus founder Walter Gropius, an example of the international style in post-war American architecture**

to form a spacious, open courtyard. Plenty of space, plenty of light, open, interconnected surfaces, access to means of transportation, and architecture built to be seen from the windows of passing cars – such things defined the new cityscapes. The same motifs cropped up all over the place: dual carriageways through the city with pedestrian bridges or underpasses; rows or dotted lines of buildings with balconies or loggias; shallow, glazed extensions for shops at the base of apartment blocks. Such were the schematically realised ideas of Le Corbusier, the Bauhaus, and Russian constructivism.

Unlikely as it seems, the socialist spirit and the architectural language of the 1920s became universal. In the process, this language gained autonomy, parting ways with the idea of socialism to champion middle-class, technocratic values and a belief in progress. The spirit of progress consisted in the idea that architecture could transform reality and the world. It determined the working method of the architect, who became a wise and benevolent surgeon fighting social and urban diseases with incisions, operation, sutures, and even amputations. One can say with some certainty that post-war modernist architecture was directly linked with socialism – via social democracy, which took on the task of transforming society and carried it out without any Bolshevist excesses.

The language of this new global architecture was not particularly complicated. The first buildings from the 1920s were inspirational in their bold simplicity and their thoroughly unconventional, Spartan handling of facades and spatial combinations. Even the most aloof observer could not but feel their effect. But post-war buildings often merged into a homogeneous mass in which individual memorable objects became almost impossible to identify. If the 30 per cent of outstanding buildings featured some exciting structural form or a particularly fine facade grid, the remaining 70 per cent were little more than plain rectangular forms. The eye of the beholder glides across the grid joints on the facades of this 70 per cent, across the smooth concrete and glass surfaces, across balconies and loggias – without anything to hold onto. All you can say is, 'Well, that's just typical post-war modernist design.'

The stark architectural language of post-war modernism spread to the applied arts, into home furnishings and book design. After the defeat of its rivals (neoclassisicm and art deco), this style became universal and absolute, dominating

8.2 **An imaginative rendering of a modernist residential district.**

all areas – from advertising signs to coffee tables and even typewriters. The more development stagnated at the core, the more vigorous was the style's overall expansion. However, the essence of modernism went beyond 'ascetic honesty' to the negation of all styles from previous epochs. The architectural austerity (as manifested in the proliferation of rectangular buildings articulated by facade grids) and the impetus to settle accounts with the past were sufficient to ensure that the new forms spread like wildfire.

The socialist states signed up to this process in the mid-1950s so thoroughly that modernism officially replaced Stalinist neoclassicism. Building projects abounded in these countries, and some of the results were formally remarkable. Yet although elements of the second wave of modernism in the USSR and the socialist states were certainly very powerful, the ambitiousness of the 1920s had waned. Many of the old constructivists did not live to experience the second wave; and even if they were still alive, almost none of them were active in a professional context. The new generation of architects made a concerted effort to 'catch up' with the West, without consciously reviving the constructivist traditions of their own countries. Russian architects in the baroque and classicist periods had found themselves in a similar situation – eternally condemned to 'catch up' with France and Italy – instead of following their own architectural traditions.

8.3 **An imaginative rendering of an urban area featuring modernist combinations of art and architecture.**

The buildings of the socialist version of modernism from the 1950s and 1960s followed the same lines as their Western counterparts. If there was a difference between them, it was that the industrially assembled, prefabricated apartment blocks (and public buildings to a lesser extent) were produced in such quantities and in such poor quality that their occupants began to loathe modernism in general. The uniform enclosures of five-storey prefabricated blocks devoid of all architectural merit acquired a symbolic quality for city dwellers. Later, even taller high-rises of the same type were introduced. Their construction was standardised, and they were distinguishable only by their serial numbers. These low-quality, standardised residential districts still feel forbidding today and fuel the aversion to modernism.

The new philosophy of urban development flooded both urban and rural housing estates with mediocre modernism. The mass production revealed the limits of modernist design as well as its aggression. The formal limitations were less palpable only in places where outstanding examples of modernist architecture at the height of its powers entered into a razor-sharp and combative dialogue with the surrounding historical remnants. For our part, we can still remember a photograph from Soviet times that appeared in every textbook: a tiny church next to a modern high-rise on Moscow's Kalinin Prospect (now Novy Arbat). This was another example of how appealing modernism could be when it created attractive contrasts through juxtaposition. If the new buildings were in a freshly developed neighbourhood with no older architecture in the vicinity, the eye quickly learned to identify the two or three types of building, the three or four types of facade grid, the five or six types of spatial combination. Such groups of uniform houses came to be as reliable a signifier of doom and gloom in the West as they had always been in the Soviet Union.

This sense of doom accompanied post-war modernism – or international modernism, as it was known – wherever it went. Apartments lost their identity and dissolved into the homogeneous mass. The battle against bourgeois homeliness resulted in monotony. New residential areas became indistinguishable from one another; Berlin and Rome were almost impossible to tell apart, and the same was true of East and West Berlin. But the most disastrous development was in the relationship between the modernist buildings and their historical surroundings. The discrepancy between modernist urban planning principles and the historical environment was so severe that in urban development terms the two not only proved incompatible but were often unable to coexist at all.

Modernism attacked the historical city. It was constantly gaining ground, intent on tearing down or destroying the old, or at least clear-cutting a path through it, biting off a chunk, as it were, and planting a new system of urban development in its place. The justification for all the invasions and demolitions was the fight against the miserable social and urban conditions of the past. The modernists argued that the old living spaces lacked light and air, and built up areas were poorly connected to arterial roads. Their main criticism of the past was, in essence, that old houses made bad living machines and that public squares were ill equipped to cope with traffic and looked overcrowded to boot. The situation called for endless interventions, new housing estates, new public buildings, new squares, and new main roads.

The interventions in the historical cityscapes were not particularly aggressive at first. Individual new builds were erected in the gaps left by bombing in the historic urban centres, which were then intersected by one or two dual carriageways, and new housing estates were built on their peripheries. But increasingly the new city would be built on top of the old and at its expense, thinning out and fraying the historical cityscape. More and more new builds were put in, organising a new type of cityscape around them (with the help of the architects, of course). The new cityscape was the polar opposite of the historical one – it was ahistorical. Time-honoured images were erased. The process was particularly heavy-handed in the cities that were worst impacted by the war and which needed rebuilding in its wake. The same applied to the new socialist cities. Berlin and Hamburg, Moscow and London, and parts of Paris saw huge areas demolished and reorganised on a vast scale. The inhabitants mourned the demolitions. They pined for the twisting lanes and the decorated houses with their gable roofs, for the old-fashioned facades with their pilasters and other ornamentation. The architects, however, were relentless.

8.4
The National Autonomous University of Mexico in Mexico City: view of the rectory with frescoes by David Alfaro Siqueiros. On the right, the Central Library with facade decoration by architect Juan O'Gorman. An example of a modernist approach to designing gigantic surface areas.

This was the first crisis of modernism: the humanitarian crisis brought on by the encounter with history, which modernism was determined to eliminate. The crisis continues to this day. International modernism is the first style that has actually attracted protest demonstrations.

The second crisis of modernism had its roots in the catastrophic lack of available forms. One could say that by the beginning of the 1960s the most important forms had been exhausted. Le Corbusier was the first to recognise that the development of the facade grid, of geometric orthogonal forms had reached a dead-end. Yet it was Le Corbusier himself who had invented the new sculptural variations of modernism. He initiated a shift in thinking from the geometry of the right angle to the geometry of the curve. Metabolists and brutalists grappled with the same crisis, albeit in very different ways, attempting to overcome it with sparse, raw sculptural forms that avoided right angles. In the brief period in which Oscar Niemeyer built the centre of Brasília with the help of Lúcio Costa, his architectural language included virtually all the smash hits and curving forms that are still in use today.

The modernist style of the 1970s (a tendency that began even earlier in parts of Western Europe, such as Germany) might be described as 'luminous' thanks to the frequent use of aluminium profile, often with a golden sheen. The coarse-mesh ornamental nets in metal or concrete that adorned the facades of residential buildings and department stores of the 1960s and 1970s also played a key role. This, too, was an attempt to introduce more complexity – not through the new geometry but through different types of materials and surfaces. The intuitive desire for filigree surface structure had spontaneously found a means of expression.

The development in the late 1960s and 1970s can be described as a constant search for forms that would lend a richer and more complex appearance, or as a permanent reformation of international modernism in the direction of greater depth and complexity. Yet this development only ever affected the 30 per cent of outstanding buildings; the remaining 70 per cent of background buildings remained as plain as ever.

But modernism's greatest crisis resulted in the brief period of postmodernism. Postmodernism was a reaction to modernism's ahistorical stance, its aggression, arrogance, and untenable aesthetic austerity. This reaction came from the ranks of the architects themselves, who, with Aldo Rossi in the

8.5 **The parliament building in Brasília, designed by Oscar Niemeyer (1960): the ensemble's distinctive silhouette is created by the convergence of large sculptural forms.**

8.6 **The presidential residence in Brasília, Palácio da Alvorada (Oscar Niemeyer, 1958), with its characteristic sculptural colonnade**

vanguard, suddenly recalled the archetypes of the historical city. The terms 'neighbourhood planning' and 'perimeter block development' returned to the urban planning lexicon. This was a critical moment in the history we are recounting because in the future, it will be the rehabilitated city district that defuses the conflict between the modernist new builds constructed in these neighbourhoods and the historical urban environment. Architects and urban planners returned to their senses and realised that a development could be subdivided into one-off architectural objects on the one hand and, on the other, the surrounding structures, which would consist of mundane buildings, often organised into perimeter block developments. Architects remembered that corner towers could be used as accents; that spheres and pyramids could crown the 30 per cent of outstanding buildings; and that columned porticos were a means to articulate and refine the surface of the facade.

These generalised forms were mechanically produced and bore none of the traces of painstaking craftsmanship. They were fashioned from plaster or concrete in bright, or even garish hues. The mechanical construction and the new materials and colours were intended to associate them with the modern era. Yet the stylistic idiom shared more motifs with architectural history than with modernism. This was a tangible step backwards, a declarative rejection of avant-garde and futuristic forms of modernism. The renunciation was not total, but it was revealing: evidently, modernism lacked sufficient forms of its own to be able to create the necessary urban diversity, and as a result, architects began looking to the past for answers, although the modernists had only just negated it. From here, it was only a small step to neoclassicism. Indeed, it underwent a revival during postmodernism and found a foothold in the United States and Great Britain, where respectable housing estates were built in historical styles, and urban mansions were designed in the style of late neoclassicism.

The main reason for the fluctuations and defeat of postmodernism was its lack of sincerity beneath the mask of irony. Irony was present in every detail and would permeate the whole building: the column capital was peculiar, the column itself might be broken or gaudily painted. Archetypal groups of forms had an erratic feel, as if drawn and built by a child. Showpiece arches did not adorn entrances to showpiece spaces. Symmetry appeared and disappeared again, as if riddled with self-doubt. But the rules governing architectural detailing were not revived. For this reason postmodernism cannot be regarded as a return to historical tradition. Rather, it was a crisis of modernism which compensated for its own lack of formal complexity by drawing on historical role models in the search for new, additional forms. One cannot help but think that such crises will be repeated if modernist austerity, particularly in the case of the 70 per cent of mundane buildings, remains the dominant approach.

In the subsequent process of development, it was important that postmodern architecture had broken with the taboo that weighed upon historical forms. Since this time, contemporary architecture has tolerated a certain degree of historicism – albeit within bounds and at the risk of being labelled kitsch as soon as there is any departure from the 'general line'. In this way postmodernism enriched contemporary architecture with new visual possibilities and new depth. Thus, in the late 1970s and early 1980s, architects could experiment with reconstructing historical cities: little glass towers, arcades, and galleries from this period are commonplace. But this style seems to demonstrate yet again that the historical texture cannot be replaced by an oversimplified language. Furthermore, it became obvious that postmodernism was merely a variation of modernism, a 'sub-style' if you will, which explains why its invasions of historical surroundings were generally perceived as disruptive or even downright aggressive. The issue was that postmodernism did not change the prevailing approach to detail but merely sought out new, grotesque forms.

By the end of the 1980s many architects had realised that postmodernism was not a 'monolith' but merely a symptom of crisis – a pathological lack of expressive forms – and that this ironic poetics of architectural archetypes had run its course. It was time to find new ways to approach modernism.

The first path that opened up was that of deconstruction, which seemed genetically related to postmodernism. A formally modernistic, technically oriented building presented itself as a literary narrative, telling a story of how it had been partly deconstructed, partly built, or even partly exploded; a capturing of a momentary state. The result was a moment of building, of demolition or explosion, preserved in stone or glass. This was new, interesting, futuristic – but suitable only for the 30 per cent of outstanding buildings that provided a rich contrast and were expensive to construct. The 70 per cent of low-cost background buildings could not afford such language.

8.7 **Hong Kong's skyline is defined by the expressive silhouettes of its various skyscrapers, a number of them in the brutalist style.**

Then modernism underwent a full-blown transformation to become neomodernism. Its formal underpinnings became a curved or rectangular grid or a building completely devoid of any facade grid – peculiar abstract sculptures that ushered in the parametric architecture of today. The traditional element of modernism, the grid, was destroyed or warped, and this proved to be the key step towards renewal. Mechanicism was largely set aside and the monotony of a machine-like rhythm was avoided in many buildings. Modernism retained all these linguistic elements and characteristics but deployed them mostly for mass construction, whereas in the 30 per cent of manifesto buildings there was an evident proclivity for bizarre shapes and supports, for surfaces with unusual contours, for forms with no historical provenance, and for a stumbling, chaotic rhythm.

A new architectural revolution has literally just taken place. The first revolution presented the new world with the 'honest', 'unadorned' architecture of cubes and grids. The second, most recent one brought with it the sculptural and irrational. Modernism put an end to the prevailing rule of symmetry and anthropomorphic proportions, while in its resurgent form it did away with rationalism once and for all and introduced proportions based on gargoyles or chimeras (as the brilliant Bernini described the work of his rival Borromini). We are witnesses of this major shift – we are experiencing how it opens up new perspectives for modernism as well as a new power of expression and a new poetics: the poetics of the harmony of contrast.

This was the birth of the genre of the unique building, a form of architecture that is highly expressive and even sculptural at times. This architecture occupies an exceptional place in art and in the public consciousness. Neither painting nor installation nor sculpture has had such an impact or so eloquently captured the mysterious and enigmatic nature of reality today and our place within it. The reason these iconic buildings are so appealing to tourists is that they are recognisable symbols of our time. They testify to a new life, informed by new technical possibilities and a new world view. These architectural monuments of today speak a grand, seemingly elite language. They are our pyramids and our tholoi.

The greatest strength of the neomodernist icons is their uniqueness, but it is also their problem. They are architectural sculptures that face their urban or rural surroundings with a sense of stark, even aggressive contrast. They occupy a critical place in the cityscape, but the city itself, in both its historic and new districts, is made up of traditional right angles. Buildings with strong expressive power contrast sharply with their urban surroundings, and this contrast is much more extreme than the juxtaposition of town houses with a baroque church ever was. This contrast between conceptual sculptural buildings and the surrounding cityscape is undeniable. One could calculate the percentage relationship between the so-called iconic buildings and their urban surroundings, for example on the main street of any city. The iconic buildings do not constitute more than 30 per cent of the overall building mass. So it might be time to reflect on how the remaining 70 per cent of background architecture might look in this age of high-contrast dialogues with ultra-modern, symbolic buildings. This is the subject of the next chapter.

8.8 **Le Volcan, the cultural centre built in 1981 by Oscar Niemeyer, is one of Le Havre's most popular tourist attractions. It stands in deliberate contrast to the orthogonal architecture of the surrounding areas designed by August Perret in the 1950s.**

Chapter 9
The Poetics of the Harmony of Contrast

When a modernistic new building has a major influence on a city and its inhabitants, by drawing in new streams of tourists for example, we speak of a 'Bilbao effect'. Frank O. Gehry's museum building in Bilbao lent this phenomenon its name, but we could mention a number of other cities and buildings that have induced a similar effect in the twentieth and twenty-first centuries. How does this happen? In Bilbao, the building created an unusual scenic phenomenon, one that from the perspective of the traditional harmony of analogy would have been altogether inconceivable some 100 years earlier, its effect predicated on the contrast that is generated with the surrounding urban landscape. For the Bilbao effect to happen, the city itself first had to emerge as an elaborate, richly detailed setting to house such a glittering diamond. A building such as this is like a firework or a brightly coloured floral arrangement set against a tasteful backdrop. There is an interesting composition by the artist Jeff Koons: a snowy white sculpture of Hercules with a small blue sphere on his shoulder. Hercules is a gigantic figure of classical beauty, but in this instance it appears as if he is only there to provide a dignified backdrop for the small blue ball. This could also be interpreted as an analogy for 'harmony in contrast', or, if you will, for the Bilbao effect.

The analogy has its limits, however. We know that a building has a function present within it. It hides behind the flowing, dynamic design of the building's shell, a design that appears as if it came out of nowhere or as if it might suddenly fall apart. The closest analogy is to a sculpture – only this sculptural work of architecture has a functional purpose.

But what historical moments do these unique structures in the urban landscape remind us of? They share the greatest similarities with the sacred buildings found in historical cities. One could say that such buildings either replace churches or are themselves churches, albeit of unusual design. We need only think of the cement churches of Gottfried Böhm, winner of the Pritzker Prize. They tower over entire neighbourhoods or even cities, dominate panoramas and skylines, create urban centres, or simply provide a point of reference – and sometimes, unfortunately, they even act as a bone of contention. We can take

9.1 A neighbourhood of old and new buildings in a historical city, generating a rich sense of contrast: an architectural fantasy

9.2 **The architectural fantasy *Two Worlds* displays the contrasts between historical and contemporary architecture.**

9.3 **View of San Pietro di Castello from the Arsenal in Venice: a typical assemblage of everyday buildings alongside outstanding architectural objects in this historical city**

9.4 Bruges: example of the shared origins of iconic and everyday architecture in a medieval city

9.5 **Honfleur, a picturesque port in Lower Normandy, is renowned for its half-timbered houses. The area around St Catherine's Church offers an example of the traditional historical integration of taller buildings into the surrounding cityscape.**

this analogy further if we think about the function of these buildings – they are most often museums (and even more often museums of modern art, meaning they are temples of the modern zeitgeist). But they could also manifest as an oceanarium, a theatre or concert hall, an art gallery, a government ministry, or the headquarters of a large company. Only very few of these sculptural structures constitute residential housing, hotels, or office buildings (other than the headquarters of large companies), for when it comes to the construction of these objects, the pragmatism of the preferred rectangular form retains its priority. But there are exceptions, such as the residential buildings designed by Zaha Hadid and Daniel Libeskind in Milan or by Stefan Behnisch for Hamburg's HafenCity.

But this temple analogy requires a certain degree of updating. Over the course of history, sacred buildings were generally the most extravagant edifices of their era. They embodied the spirit of the age as well as contemporary notions of timelessness. In this regard, the sculptural buildings of modern Western cities are indeed similar to a place of worship: they too represent the sum of all the prevailing ideas about the innovative potentials of modern architecture as well as its faith in the future. In the past, however, a church, a palace, a tower, or a city hall would have stood at the top of the architectural hierarchy and was thus an accumulation of all the architectural achievements of its age. Generally, a church was sited on high ground and surrounded by less sophisticated structures – and these structures became more and more modest as one moved towards the edge of the city.

In other words, from the background buildings to the crystal-like qualities of the house of worship, the architecture became increasingly complex, while at its core it remained unchanged, merely enriching itself with new technologies and methods. We describe this as a harmony of analogy, for one finds this parallel in the design and proportions of both the simple buildings and the outstanding edifices of the era. If the house of worship as a city's architectural highpoint was replaced by a royal residence, a town hall, or a museum, these buildings then held the same position in the urban landscape. They thereby maintained the architectural forms of their age, refined them, or took them to monumental proportions. The architectural hierarchy, however, remained unchanged. Numerous violations of this rule took place in

the 1920s, when there was a growing tendency to build forms that strongly contrasted with their historical setting. The socialist workers' clubs of the 1920s, residential housing, and public buildings created an active contrast with the historical cityscape. These works represented a declaration of the new and a break with tradition. Here one only need think of Melnikov's Moscow clubs and the house he built for himself.

If we examine current examples of architecture that stand in contrast to their surroundings, we see that the hierarchy of the similar, the analogy, in other words, has come permanently undone. The situation might look something like this: in the middle of a city stands a building that has accumulated the entire complexity of the most up-to-date architectural thinking. It is filled with forms, ideas, references, and allusions. In formal terms, this is all part of modernism and the avant-garde. Allusions, references, and associations primarily arise from avant-garde, modernist forms and their history. We find ourselves confronted with a truly modern architecture which apparently only refers to itself and is replete with memories recalling its own intellectual origins. It acknowledges no deeper past, nor does it refer back to the abundance of pre-modern architectural forms. It can thus be either sculpturally complex or provocatively minimalist.

This type of building – the building as sculpture, as work of art, or as minimalist icon – is not integrated into the historic squares, streets, and neighbourhoods (much as the architectural advisory boards like to call for these buildings to be inserted into the urban landscape, their demands are difficult for truly modern architecture to comply with!). These sculptural buildings are not embedded in the traditional harmony of the homogeneous or the transmission of old techniques. Their entire nature rebels against any attempt to incorporate them or make them fit in with their surroundings, for they follow completely different principles of composition. These buildings find themselves in an active, contradictory dialogue with the city. In this sense, they are buildings of contention, of counterpoint.

Here we are dealing with a new reality. We must take note of this reality and try to understand its potential advantages arising from a new kind of harmony: a harmony of contrast. A building of maximal complexity challenges the entire city, first and foremost the surrounding architecture, both old and new. It manifests its individuality, uniqueness, and value; it

9.6
The home of the architect Melnikov in Moscow is an example of the deliberate contrast of an object to its surroundings – here to the typical buildings of the Arbat District.

displays its complexity and overwhelms us with its virtuosity or an asceticism that is deliberately taken to an extreme. However, it does not blend with the city or lend its surroundings any of its own complexity and aesthetics; nor does it let itself be influenced by the aesthetics of its immediate surroundings.

Viewed as consciously outstanding, the status of these buildings can be compared to that of the intellectual maverick: these individuals, too, lead isolated lives far apart from one another. They express their thoughts in the same distant fashion, and their utterances have the power to abruptly transform everything around them. Together they form a community, but only rarely do they have anything to do with one another – in the pages of learned journals perhaps. They operate and live in a different world, a world of ideas and percepts, and they differ in that regard from everyone else.

One could say that the highlights of great architecture spur each other on to ever more powerful statements. One could also say that the architecture of our time has split, leaving us faced with two kinds of architecture: manifesto architecture, which presents truths or makes very simple statements (as in rhetorical or prophetic architecture), and architecture for the background, which has no voice of its own (or just regurgitates platitudes). In this artistic interplay, the latter, the background architecture, may be devoid of any artistic quality. But this is of no importance, because no one notices it. It exists outside of aesthetics in the realm of the everyday object.

One could also say that it has always been this way, even before the arrival of modernism. It is true that there has always been top-class architecture whose purpose was to make 'statements' and create core ideas and forms. And there has always been a background architecture that borrows or incorporates these forms. Design ideas have been continuously passed down from the heights of manifesto architecture to the lowlands of serial construction and the broad base of the periphery, and in the process they have been increasingly watered down and simplified. In this regard, everything is as it has always been.

But this is simply not the case. The architecture of the past did not experience such tremendous aesthetic discrepancies between an epoch's dominant architecture and its surroundings, which were characterised by its austere, mechanistic, and pragmatic forms and methods. This explains why the

new, truly progressive architecture is so radical in its renunciation and contrast to the old-established surroundings. For ideological reasons these buildings lost their connection to the historical backdrop, and they no longer have anything aesthetically in common with modern, pragmatic, mass architecture.

Victory in the war against the totalitarian neoclassicist style and in a further battle with postmodernism, accompanied, most importantly, by the opening up of fundamentally new possibilities in the field of parametric modelling in planning and construction, paved the way for a new form of architecture with sculptural and sometimes rather eccentric forms. This is clearly an exclusive form of architecture due to the high construction costs associated with it. It claims to express the ideas and emotions of our era. It keeps pace with modern art, which is ever more sculpturally complex and continues to favour the installation and polyphony. This iconographic architecture is now capable of expressing complex or even extremely complex statements in a language of increasingly elaborate and technically expert solutions. And society, too, has begun to listen to these architectural statements, even though they may run counter to expectations, in the hope that they will provide something new. These are the times in which we live, and they have quite a long history of their own. The history of modernism began 100 years ago as an artistic revolution. This revolution destroyed and swept away conventional, classical figuration that no one believed would ever die. Many welcomed the change, and to this day there is a palpable enthusiasm for it among artists in general. But the devastation proved unbearable for normal observers of architecture, who were used to its graphic qualities: their craving for visual detail was so great that they could not accept its fall from grace and steady demise. In the realm of art, figuration found refuge in books and cinema and has now found a new home in the internet. It was never really lost – it is just that it has completely, or almost completely, disappeared from the lofty heights of the artistic world.

Something similar also occurred in architecture. Figuration disappeared along with the classical order, the decorations, the reliefs, and the ornamentation. Architecture's leading edge is now all about provocation and radical dialogue, and the periphery has been permeated by a faceless, pragmatic form of minimalism bereft of all beauty (a concept that architecture has entirely forgotten!).

9.7 **The ArtScience Museum and the Marina Bay Sands Hotel are the dominant architectural works that define the sculptural appearance of the cityscape of modern Singapore.**

The result is that we now find ourselves confronted with the following situation: the intellectuals at the top with their refined sense of form and material offer their new creations to the world, but these creations find no artistically adequate setting once they are displaced from the historical setting and inserted into the realm of contemporary background architecture.

Design solutions developed for architectural icons are of course actively integrated into contemporary mass architecture to a certain extent. These design characteristics and devices can be found in buildings of all sizes and functions. When the newest forms shift from being highlights of the built environment to becoming part of the mass of more widespread (and, it should be noted, cheaper) architecture, they are not adapted to the urban environment as was typical with the 'hierarchical' style: background buildings with novel forms pose a contrast to their surroundings, just like the antecedents they are modelled on. The effect is no longer that of a jewel or architectural icon embedded in a less exalted yet contextually equal chain of precious stones. Quite the opposite, in fact, for the result is an annoying confusion of voices. It is as if one neighbour were trying to shout down all the others.

Buildings with novel forms do not speak a common language: they conflict with one another, and this is why an urban area made up of 'adapted', simplified examples of architecture from the recent past appears as a cacophony in material form. The buildings 'jostle' and scream confusedly at each other. They wrangle for dominance.

It is immediately obvious that this cannot become the new normal. The last thing we want is for our world to be seen as an anti-utopia in the making. But the truth is that a passionate architectural movement has upset the balance. The avant-garde was pioneering in that it had a major impact on other styles, but it had no idea how to deal with everyday life and how it should harmonise with its own surroundings, which it is particularly poor at: an architectural environment that has a primitive sense of pragmatism can contribute nothing to such harmonisation. If our analysis of the situation is correct, then one might try to offer a solution, a way to redesign urban neighbourhoods, squares, and new residential areas. The background architecture would inevitably live on – in the shadow of the outstanding architecture it contrasts with.

These background buildings remain virtually unobserved by critics and members of the public alike and go more or less unnoticed – a great deal can and must be done in this regard, for everything that is designed and realised in this area has an impact on a major portion of the urban landscape, the 70 per cent of buildings that we have identified. The new and outstanding architecture that makes up the other 30 per cent continues to make great waves, and it is possible for a new understanding of figurative architecture to be developed for the remaining 70 per cent of simpler structures – as part of modern culture. This would lead to a new background architecture that can stand alongside the sculptural works of architecture. It could offer an answer to all the provocations and challenges of manifesto buildings, be they refined or minimalistic, cubic in form or entirely without straight lines and angles.

Today's architecture has endured the modernism that spanned the period from the 1950s to the 1970s. It let off as much steam as it wanted during the era of postmodern self-irony in the 1980s before returning to the well-trodden paths of modernism in the 1990s. It has, one might believe, lived through every phase in its examination of the so-called pure form, which is free of all ornamentation and figuration. In doing so, it has put itself at some considerable distance – perhaps beyond the point of no return – from the once fundamental argument calling for the renunciation of all forms of ornament (epitomised by the well-known adage 'form follows function'). Today's approaches to form and surface are, as in all previous epochs – and this is a point that we have repeatedly sought to stress – attempts at an artistic understanding of architectural volume, which only has a limited amount to do with its function.

If we try to systematise the most important methods that have defined the style of contemporary architecture, we come upon five 'types' of approach to form and surface that are found in the overwhelming majority of recent buildings.

Type 1

The structural framework is made visible and filled in with a different material. The facade's structural net, which may (or may not) have something to do with the true supporting structure, can be rectangular (or not). It can be filled in entirely with glass (or not).

9.8 The architectural fantasy *City of Contrasts II* illustrates how the cultural layers of the 19th, 20th, and 21st centuries coexist in the modern city.

Sometimes a transparent or semi-transparent meshwork, with a more or less outlandish form, is stretched over the framework. This layer is known as a double-skin facade.

Type 2

The building's mass is made visible. Differently from Type 1, a massive volume is clad in any desired material with openings that can be rectangular or non-rectangular, large or small, and arranged in a regular or irregular pattern. In some instances, when the volume is a cube, the corners can be cut off at a random angle or rounded in order to accentuate the building's expressive power, which inevitably draws comparisons to the buildings of Erich Mendelsohn or the Russian constructivists, who are often cited as a reference in this context.

Type 3

The building's form retains a more or less geometrically clear character, which makes the primary volume recognisable as such. Individual rectangular or intentionally non-rectangular elements are then added. These elements can be a three-dimensional continuation of the facade pattern (oblique or symmetrical three-dimensional pylons and crossbars) or projecting or recessed bay windows of any shape.

Type 4.

The constructional volume is articulated and transformed into a geometric sculpture with console-like projecting and sunken elements in the form of cubes, trapezoids, triangles, or even curves. This type originated in cubist painting and the collages of Vladimir Tatlin. It may appear in solid (Type 2) or glazed (Type 1) facades.

Type 5.

The bionic or crystal-like sculpture is characterised by the complete or nearly complete absence of rectangles in the design. Volumes are either created by means of a combination of broken lines or based on curved structures. This type is typically found in the best-known iconic buildings, but it is also adopted by less prominent structures.

All of these types are characteristic of the architecture that is supposed to symbolise today's culture. It best coexists with the culture of the past as a contrasting element – if, that is, a stroke of luck has placed the architecture of the past nearby, thus helping the new architecture to stand out against the background. It is precisely by virtue of this contrast to the historical backdrop, and at its expense, that iconographical architecture is able to draw the largest crowds of admirers. But what happens when the historical architecture is absent and the new ensemble is to be applied to an empty canvas? This is something we would like to examine here in more detail.

If we look at the most well-known historical cities, in Europe for example, we find that a district made up of, say, 100 buildings whose facades are decorated in the style that was prevalent at the time they were built will boast no more than 30 buildings that occupy a special place in the architectural framework. These 30 buildings are churches, administrative buildings, theatres, the mansions of the wealthy, commercial architecture whose owners are vying for attention, and, finally, corner buildings that give the neighbourhood a distinctive quality. Today we would describe these buildings as icons, and in the past their task was the creation not only of an impressive street facade but also of a three-dimensionally impressive volume, for such buildings generally stood on their own, framed by streets and squares, or on a corner property at the end of a visual axis, or they would establish their own spatial compositions in a street lined with buildings.

Today's architecture can erect these 30 buildings according to the five types of formal design described above, and these buildings command a degree of attention that is proportional to the amount of contrast between the new buildings and their mundane surroundings. However, if a historical environment is not present, a fundamental problem arises: modern architecture is no longer able to create a visually satisfying urban environment whose quality is on a par with that of the streetscapes of the past. But the relationship that we have defined for historical cities can equally be applied to modern cities: here, too, the ratio of 30:70 appeals to our imagination as a symbol of the harmony of contrast.

But we are not finished yet. In the universities, architects are trained to become the star architects who will design these 30 from the set of 100 buildings. But who will build the other 70? What creative tools will they use? No one knows the answer to these questions at present. Critics believe that background architecture that refuses to be minimalist represents a compromise and even a form of kitsch, but the fact remains that no one would think to call cities beautiful whose architecture only consists of the five types described above. At best, we might describe them as interesting, daring, modern, or, more often than not, boring and depressing. This can be traced directly back to the inability to create an urban backdrop that is rich in details – as a crucial and worthy setting for every remarkable building in the urban landscape. Today's architecture is capable of establishing a minimalist or bionic contrast to its historical surroundings, in the form of a conceptual or sculptural building in line with the types listed above, which, in turn, can best coexist with these surroundings by evoking contrast. But what will happen to the gigantic modern residential areas and cities? It is impossible for these to consist only of bionic or minimalistic buildings seeking to provide contrast. But this is exactly the situation we find ourselves faced with, and this is precisely why such buildings will never arouse our enthusiasm. The only way out of this situation is as follows: we should learn once again – and then teach the construction industry – how to create urban landscapes and, in so doing, utilise a broad palette of details, be they newly developed or borrowed, while ensuring at all costs that the new urban landscapes include more appealing, graceful facades for the mundane background buildings. The challenge for town planners is to find preferential locations for the 30 per cent of outstanding objects within the frameworks of their master plans and the predetermined development structures. The purpose of all the other buildings is to form the urban environment, and they require significant improvements in the shape of an abundance of appealing details and a more refined facade structure, for aside from the surface of their facades, they have nothing of note to offer. Indeed, that is all that is required of them.

9.9 **The corner tower of a 19th-century building is a dominant highlight in the historical urban landscape.**

Chapter 10
The 30:70 Principle as a Balance of Power

In the previous chapters we attempted to explain what it was that modernist architecture in the twentieth century consciously determined to renounce: high density of detail on the surface of a building. We have tried to depict how historical architectural development was fundamentally about the evolution of surface ornamentation, namely embellishments, decorations, and reliefs. Construction techniques and building materials also developed and changed, of course, but nonetheless the assigning of a building to a particular epoch or style was primarily based on the way it was decorated.

Modern buildings, deprived of a wealth of possibilities for decorative expression, have lost their former richness of detail but have gained a number of options for formal creativity. For architects, these possibilities constituted the principle and technical guidelines for the construction of the new architecture. In chapter 9 we organised these possibilities into five types. Some will say that these types represent the modern architectural orders, whereas others might claim that they represent hackneyed clichés introduced during the twentieth century.

Likewise, the historical Greco-Roman order served as guide for a great many architects for centuries. However, this could be applied not only to temples and palaces – that is to say, for the outstanding 30 per cent of buildings – but also to more humble structures, all similar in appearance, which effortlessly created the urban landscapes of the past.

What happens when a modern building is erected in a historical architectural environment? It always stands in contrast to its surroundings. Even in instances in which a modern building attempts to adapt and 'blend in' – as is vainly demanded of it in many countries by architectural experts and building regulations – it will always stand out irredeemably against its historical neighbours thanks to its minimalism (to use the language of architects) or plainness of surface (to use the language of the everyday user) as well as the mechanistic rhythm and simplified articulation of its facades. Yes, it is the facades of all things that are the key here, for despite the large number of geometric and bionic sculptural buildings, most property investors and users find it easiest to construct plain rectangular buildings with facades – which over the course of their history were always decorated, until this was declared an expression of bad taste some 100 years ago.

When there are historical buildings nearby, the new buildings-as-objects drawn from the five types described above can stand next to one another and present a rather colourful picture that has very little to do with the ensembles of the past that we know from Saint Petersburg, Paris, and Rome. However, a string of new buildings does not add up to an ensemble that draws upon contrast to create harmony. What is missing from this juxtaposition of buildings is an elegant chain of modest yet finely detailed facades that can offer a background setting in which an architectural (and hopefully genuine) jewel can shine. Even if we could decree that on top of the 70 per cent of buildings making up the modern urban landscape – which are plain and mechanistic by virtue of the restraint imposed on them – come the 30 per cent of more unusual buildings, the wonder of contrasting harmony

would still fail to manifest itself, because the necklace designed to hold our jewels would prove to be nothing more than 'dull tin'. So what is to be done? The approach or word of advice with which we would like to conclude this book will be rather simple. But first, before we offer this advice or specify the recipe, we would like to return to the question of who this book was written for.

We are not seeking to address those people who believe that historical cities can only be filled with historically stylised buildings. Again and again the authors of this book have discussed this point with proponents of this idea: Is it possible to imagine a beautiful, highly modern building standing alongside a pearl of the Saint Petersburg imperial style, an iconic building by Carlo Rossi? Naturally it was impossible for us to reach consensus on this point.

Nor is this book aimed at readers who find absolutely nothing wrong with the development of contemporary architecture and do not find the sight of rows of heterogeneous works of modern architecture in any way disturbing or disharmonious. After all, we have the Ginza district in Tokyo and new neighbourhoods in Amsterdam or Oslo that were built according to this principle. For how long will they continue to delight observers? Is it even necessary for contemporary architecture to make longevity a goal?

Instead, this book is aimed at all of those who share our conviction that architecture was created not simply to last for decades. It should stand for centuries. We are writing this book for people who, like us, recognise that contemporary architecture can scale the heights within the framework of a single project, and that in pursuit of this it has at its disposal technical capabilities that were inconceivable only a few years ago. However, this does not mean that they are capable of consciously contributing to a new ensemble that lives from the harmony of contrast.

In this ensemble we would allocate 30 per cent to buildings constructed using untried methods and with a great deal of talent and diligence, for these are the buildings that take on the important role of the 'troublemaker'. They take up all of the attention of those viewers who, we would hope, find the ensemble a source of wonder rather than of loathing.

10.1 **The coexistence of contemporary and background buildings: an architectural fantasy**

10.2 A richly detailed historical setting for the sculptural form of a contemporary bridge: an architectural fantasy

These buildings can make themselves stand out from their surroundings in terms of both height and ground plan, they can tower above the neighbouring structures or cut through them, and, based on the materials used in their construction, they can set up a contrast with the background architecture, a setting that proves itself worthy of them.

And we would dedicate 70 per cent to those buildings that surround the architectural objects (qua manifestos) – or icons, as they are so often described – acting as a kind of jewelled necklace. This type of urban environment is something that architects are now no longer able to design. Or it is something they do with a great deal of effort and wariness. These types of buildings are not to be found among the five types we have described, for all five are lacking in restraint when it comes to the building's form and the refinement of its surface, which is such a key element: this refinement is achieved by means of details, depth of relief, and ornamentation, or by giving the surface a haptic quality. What we are talking about is the very means of embellishment that architects of all people so fear: ornament and decoration – basically everything that could make the surfaces of contemporary buildings as rich in variety as those found on historical buildings.

Only when, in the handling of the facade structure – regardless of whether this is the result of drawing upon the old architectural orders or by means of newly developed structures, ornamentation, and reliefs – the necessary density is achieved to allow the facade to be viewed from up close and to age with dignity, only then can we, in our opinion, expect buildings with such facades to become both worthy elements in the cityscape and participants in the urban spectacle (based as it is on the principle of the harmony of contrast), thus incorporating the entire bandwidth of contemporary architectural expression into the way our cities look.

This harmony of contrast is based upon something which Renaissance politicians referred to as the 'balance of power'. In the fragmented Italy of the sixteenth century, politicians attempted a complex balancing act by entering into alliances with small and medium-sized states, whereby a certain degree of military and political equilibrium had to be assured. Here, we wish to transfer the term 'balance of power' to the realm of architecture, to equilibrium in the urban landscape. Once again, 30 per cent is allotted to outstanding buildings, and 70 per cent to the surrounding urban architecture.

We are convinced that a dynamic balance can be created in the urban landscape in which residents will feel at ease, not too flustered (if, for instance, the iconic buildings were to exceed their share), and not too apathetic (if the mass development were to gain the upper hand).

We believe modern architecture represents a field in which two forces must maintain equilibrium relative to one another – the provocative manifesto buildings and the urban backdrop. We are well aware that our suggested ratio of 30:70 is rather imprecise as a proportion that can be used to enable cities to maintain their integrity without becoming atomised or transforming into a faceless mass (which would happen, and indeed does happen, if the ratio is not maintained). We are talking about a proportion that can be applied to the new urban ensemble, about coexistence for different kinds of buildings, whereby no one style is allowed to gain the upper hand. The goal, rather, is a balance of 30:70, a balance which guarantees, in our opinion, the harmony of contrast we have described. A disruption of this balance leads to the disappearance of this delicate harmony. The majority buildings should continue to play an important role in this newly conceived ensemble. Just as the setting of a ring connects the jewel with its wearer, the urban environment's task is to ground the entire architectural composition and give it a human scale. This is why the numerous buildings of the background not only require facade surfaces that are richly detailed but should also have physical dimensions that are designed with people in mind. We believe that rows of buildings with an average of six storeys, with high ceilings of at least 3 metres, street facade lengths of 20 to 30 metres per building, and sloping roofs will cause the unattractive still lifes to be found in engineered structures to finally disappear from every modern city panorama and create a humane, people-friendly urban environment.

If the majority of buildings in a given city are of this height, and if they stand across from one another at a distance of 25 metres, this would ensure a pleasant width. The height of the background buildings would also contribute to creating an exciting, attractive contrast between the urban setting and the individual examples of outstanding buildings. Such buildings can and must tower above their surroundings or stand on city squares or at major road junctions, at times set back at a greater distance from the building line. At any rate, they

10.3 **Detailing on the facades in Venice's Castello neighbourhood near the church of Santa Maria Formosa (left)**

10.4 **The Amalfi Cathedral and an adjacent alleyway with medieval buildings showing a rich variety of decorative features (right)**

should be erected at prominent locations in the urban land-scape so that they have optimal visibility and can be viewed from the greatest possible distance. In the urban panorama, the silhouettes of these iconic buildings would stand out against the buildings below them, thus creating an unforget-table skyline characteristic of the individual city.

There is one factor inherent to any theatrical production that would not bode well for an urban setting: every play must end. We are convinced, however, that the urban ensem-ble must be capable of generating joy and wonder over a very long period. That is why buildings must display a particular quality that has yet to appear in our typologies: the building should be able to age with dignity, not only in terms of its materials, but spiritually as well.

This quality of dignified aging is particularly important for the buildings in the background. After all, these structures are in the majority (as we have said many times, they make up 70 per cent of the city); they form the urban fabric, and if they are replaced every 20, 30, or even 50 years (when it comes to the history of the city and the history of architec-ture, these might as well be seconds), this means not only that the work and energy of the builders are set at naught but also that the city's 'cultural layers' are constantly being erased for generations to come. After all, the more layers that exist, the more interesting the city's appearance.

For the icons – the outstanding buildings – aging, even spiritual aging, is not as problematic. They are fewer in num-ber, and we can assume that in their planning and construc-tion the most up-to-date technologies were used, and the investments were much higher than for the majority of buildings. Both the construction and the facades (or shell) of these buildings are much more complex. They often house important social institutions and thus receive more atten-tion and funds for maintenance and renovation. Their moral aging is not that dramatic, for the general perception of these buildings persists: they are the greatest achievements of the culture of their age. Of course, it can happen that an icon is torn down after only a few decades – we need only think of the dismantling and recently completed second rebuilding of Les Halles in Paris, once known as the 'belly of Paris'. If architectural icons are renovated, this can some-times be amazingly expensive, as was the case with the Centre Pompidou.

The surrounding buildings, on the other hand, have to take care of themselves if they wish to survive. No one would invest in the renovation of the seemingly soulless concrete-grid facades typical of the residential and office buildings of the 1960s and 1970s. And if the old buildings of Saint Petersburg and Lviv, Rome, and Barcelona remain wonderfully beautiful to this day, even though they are in desperate need of renova-tion, then this can be put down to their diverse, gracefully aging facade structures. They steadfastly bear all the hard-ships of aging with dignity and a degree of grace that today's urban buildings will find rather difficult to imitate.

This is why when designing modern urban buildings (which have been our constant focus throughout this text), we must initially forgo all the motifs that appear so fashionable today but have nothing to do with building tectonics and are there-fore, like every fashion accessory, short-lived. Such motifs include the window rhythms that are offset floor by floor, non-orthogonal window openings, and a number of other artistic devices that every contemporary architect knows and uses in order to appear modern, despite the fact that these design tricks conflict with the logic of the static distribution of weight on the facade. The structurally unfounded facades are all well and good when it comes to iconic buildings, and even then, only if they are truly new and unusual. For the majority of buildings they appear unnatural and inappropriate.

But even more important when it comes to physical and spiritual aging is the building material itself. The wonderful old buildings we spoke of above were built of solid brickwork without any additional insulation but with ornamentation, stucco, or brick decoration that was itself part of the support-ing wall. In all of the cases described, the decoration is neces-sary and achieves its aim: dust collects on the reliefs to create a patina, and this allows their sculptural design to become visible in a way that can be planned in advance, contributing to an effect that lasts for many years. The faces of these his-torical buildings age over time, and only in the worst instances do they crumble into picturesque ruins.

In the case of modern buildings, it is not their face that decays but a mask that is not connected to the character of the build-ing itself. Nearly all contemporary buildings include an unat-tractive facade layer of insulating panels. An additional layer is applied on top of this insulating material – stone, ceramic, cement boards, or even plaster. The material is so thin that it

10.5 **The wealth of details on the facade surface of a simple house in Taormina**

10.6 **Section of the architectural decoration for a doorway in Venice**

looks like wallpaper, and it can peel off just as easily. This reveals not the fine brickwork of a century ago but instead rotten, matted panels of insulating material.

What is to be done? Building technologies must be fundamentally changed and new ones developed. Energy-saving regulations today are especially strict, but we must nevertheless design solid external walls of economically affordable strength that are capable of supporting or of being transformed into a nuanced upper layer that fragments and refines the surface of the facade. Industrial manufacturers at present are not confronted with this task, because no one seems to care about the poor quality and rapid decay of the architecture of the urban environment. But these buildings form the skeleton of the city

we will inhabit in the future, and our descendants will take them as a measure by which to judge the construction technologies and architectural culture of our era.

Closing Remarks

We have viewed architectural history as an evolution of styles by examining the evolution of its graphic ornamentation. Our focus was on architecture and the architect as an artist whose own stylistic variations reflect the time he lived in. It was important for us to show that architects of every era up until the early twentieth century were capable not only of constructing a building but also of designing it. For if there was only room in architecture for constructors or inventors working on large-scale forms, then where did that leave the artists who were focused on smaller-scale designs? We are convinced that architecture's graphic nature has much to do with the fact that the majority of everyday buildings are or should be of lasting artistic value.

We have shown how and why modernism bid farewell to figuration as well as which means of expression (sculptural, dynamic, contrast-oriented, minimalist) were developed by the best, programmatic aspect of modern architecture. In this process, architects may have lost something, but they also made substantial gains thanks to the fundamentally new design resources that were now at their disposal. However, it also meant that the temptation to exclusively focus on creating original buildings was so great that every architect strove to build the 30 per cent allotted to this 'architecture of contrast' in urban landscapes. And hardly anyone is interested in consciously applying themselves to designing nuanced architecture for the urban setting, which, in our opinion, should comprise the absolute majority of buildings – the 70 per cent. This has led to a situation in which a city's background architecture is synonymous with the nondescript architecture that is primarily aimed at utilitarian purposes, makes no attempt at artistic solutions, and is therefore incapable of entering into a restrained yet self-assured dialogue with works of manifesto architecture.

We have shown both the potentials and the shortcomings of today's urban landscapes, which – almost subconsciously, we believe – attempt to organise themselves according to the rules of the harmony of contrast. In this modern ensemble there is a potential centre, an interface, or a hub, but what is missing today is the setting, the jewelled necklace, the background. Creating this background is something that has to be learned so that the harmony of contrast can be developed, supported, and maintained.

We would argue in favour of reclaiming the historically proven advantages offered by figurative sculpturality and a high degree of detailing for the facades of urban streetscapes. Doing so will allow the harmony of contrast in new urban ensembles to attain the quality found in the positive examples to be found in the historical streetscapes of European cities where we find the new and the old coexisting harmoniously.

We would also like to stress the great importance of detail for every building, regardless of whether it offers a point of contrast or exists in the background. The saliency of the form or the accentuation of a part of a spatial composition should not result in the neglect of the detailing or quality of the surfaces. Complexity, simplicity, and particular features of the composition should be balanced by intensive detailing, for if the impact of the composition is global, the effect of the detailing also makes itself felt on a more local, human scale. And only when composition and detail are balanced and elaborated to the same extent can they work together to form a new ensemble. When they approach a building, observers should receive new emotional stimuli that encourage them to take in all of its surface details – just as our eye sates itself by drinking in all the beauty of the crown of a tree viewed from a distance, before moving closer to see the formal beauty of its individual leaves.

We deliberately offer no practical recipes for how our urban surroundings are to be constructed but instead point out the shortcomings and symptoms of the absence of such recipes and indicate ways in which these might be remedied by means of a radical densification of the message inscribed in the facade surface and, thus, a focus on the longevity that can be achieved in this way.

Neither figuration nor, for that matter, material haptics are taught much to architects nowadays. No time is given to these subjects, for they are considered nothing more than old-fashioned kitsch. But we believe that concrete methods in the service of new graphic qualities and detailing must be developed by creatively reordering, assimilating, and utilising all the knowledge to be found in the history of global architecture. This constitutes a broad field with significant scope for actively developing an architecture that caters to the entirety of the urban landscape.

And for our readers we hope that the ways of approaching architecture that they discover in this book may offer insights into what can be done to make the profane, simple buildings in our urban environment more beautiful and likeable.

Index of Names

The *Deutsche Bibliothek* lists this publication in the *Deutsche Nationalbibliografie*; detailed bibliographic data is available on the Internet at *http://dnb.d-nb.de*

ISBN 978-3-86922-683-5

© 2017 by New Literary Observer Publishing House, Moscow
www.nlobooks.ru

Title of the original Russian edition of this book:
Сергей Чобан, Владимир Седов
30:70. Архитектура как баланс сил

© 2018 by DOM publishers, Berlin
www.dom-publishers.com

Translation and copy-editing
Tradukas GbR

Proofreading
Kristin Feireiss

Editing
Tatiana Beliakova

Drawings
Sergei Tchoban

Design concept
Masako Tomokiyo

Layout
Dmitriy Sadovnikov

Printing
Tiger Printing (Hong Kong) Co., Ltd.
www.tigerprinting.hk

DOM publishers